SCRATCH YOUR BRAIN
GEOMETRY

MATH GAMES, TRICKS, AND QUICK ACTIVITIES

SERIES TITLES:
SCRATCH YOUR BRAIN A1
SCRATCH YOUR BRAIN B1
SCRATCH YOUR BRAIN C1
SCRATCH YOUR BRAIN ALGEBRA

DOUG BRUMBAUGH
DAVID ROCK

Graphic Design by
Danielle West

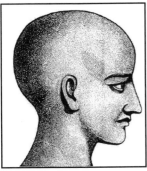

© 2006
THE CRITICAL THINKING CO.
(BRIGHT MINDS™)
www.criticalthinking.com
P.O. Box 1610 • Seaside • CA 93955-1610
ISBN 0-89455-908-7

CONTENTS —————————————————

2 & 3 DIMENSIONAL OBJECTS ———

1. The apex of a pyramid is the vertex where the triangular faces meet. A pyramid is isosceles if the apex is equidistant from all vertices of the base. Write an explanation of why the base of an isosceles pyramid is inscribed in a circle which is centered at the foot of the pyramid's altitude.

2. A cone has a radius of r units and a height of h units. A cylinder has a radius of 2r units and has the same volume as the cone. What is the height of the cylinder? Write an explanation of how you got your answer.

3. A cube has pyramids (tetrahedrons) cut from each corner by passing planes through the midpoints of the edges adjacent to each vertex of the cube. Each pyramid is discarded and a new solid remains. How many edges would the new solid have? Note that the picture shows only one of the tetrahedron cuts. Write an explanation of how you arrived at your answer.

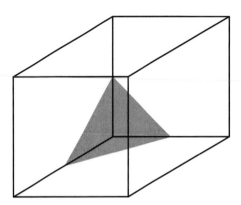

4. You are given a 5 cm by 12 cm rectangle ABCD. How many distinct circles in the same plane of the rectangle have a diameter both of whose endpoints are vertices of rectangle ABCD? What is the sum of the diameters of all of the circles? Write an explanation of how you got your answer.

5. Inscribe congruent circles in each of a regular triangle, square, pentagon, hexagon, and decagon. What conclusion can be made about the areas of each circumscribed polygon as the number of sides increases? Write an explanation of how you got your answer.

6.   The interior angles of a regular polygon measure 156°. How many sides does the polygon have? Explain in writing how you got your answer. Try to solve this problem at least two different ways.

7.   Quadrilateral ABCD is a square with area of 256 square units. Triangle CEF is a right triangle (angle FCE is right) with area of 200 square units. Find the length of segment BE. Write an explanation of how you got your answer.

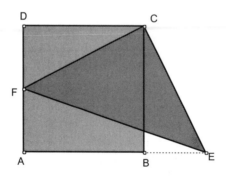

8.   A convex polygon has 324 diagonals. How many sides does this polygon have?
     Write an explanation of how you got your answer.

9.   A triangle is drawn pointing upward (one vertex at the top and two vertices at
     the bottom). The midpoints of its three sides are connected with line segments
     forming a smaller triangle inside the initial triangle. The midpoints of the sides
     of this smaller triangle are again connected with line segments. This process is
     repeated one more time. Now shade all small triangles pointing upward. What
     is the fractional part of the original triangle that is shaded? Write an explanation
     of how you got your answer.

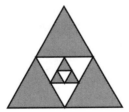

10. You are given 9 segments whose lengths are 1 cm, 2 cm, 3 cm, . . . , 9 cm respectively. If you chose three segments at random, what is the probability that the three segments will be able to form a triangle?

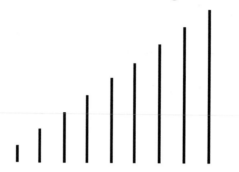

11. The parallel sides of a trapezoid are 3 units and 9 units while the nonparallel sides are 4 units and 6 units. A segment is drawn parallel to the bases and that segment divides the original trapezoid into two smaller trapezoids having the same perimeter. What is the ratio into which each of the nonparallel sides is divided? Write an explanation of how you got your answer.

12.   1) In any triangle, the sum of the lengths of the three altitudes is greater than the semi-perimeter of that triangle.
2) In any triangle, the sum of the lengths of the three medians is greater than the semi-perimeter of that triangle.
3) In any triangle, the sum of the measures of the three angle bisectors (terminated at the respective opposite side) is greater than the semi-perimeter of that triangle.

Which of 1, 2, and 3 are always true, and which are always false? Prove your answer.

Note: Semi-perimeter is half the perimeter of the figure.

13.   A farmer wants to buy a plot of ground adjacent to currently owned property. A real estate agent says the triangular plot has side lengths 30, 45, and 85 decameters. The land costs $17.99 per square decameter. Knowing that Heron's formula can be used to compute the area of any triangle, how much did the farmer pay for the ground? Write an explanation of how you got our answer. Heron's formula: Area = $\sqrt{s(s - a)(s - b)(s - c)}$, where a, b, and c are the triangle side lengths and s = $\dfrac{a + b + c}{2}$.

14. Three unit circles are mutually tangent. There is a circle inscribed in the central region created by the three larger circles. This little circle is tangent to the other three. What is the radius of this little inscribed circle?

15. The diameter of the circle centered at A is 8 units. The length of $\overline{BE}$ is 3 units and $\angle ABF$ is a right angle. What is the length of segment $\overline{BC}$?

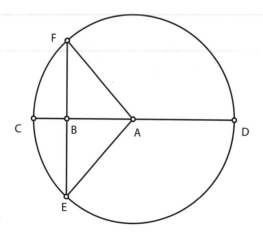

16.   Suppose the earth is a sphere and its circumference at the equator is 25,000 miles. Imagine a ring that forms a band around the earth. The circumference of the ring is 25,000 miles PLUS 10 feet. The ring and the equator are concentric (share the same center) circles. What is the distance between the equator and the ring? Write an explanation of how you got your answer.

17.   One base of the trapezoid is 8 units and the other is 18 units. What is the diameter of the inscribed circle?

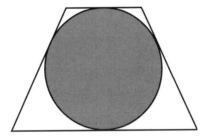

18. Two chords in the same circle are perpendicular to each other. The point of intersection divides one chord into segments of 3 and 4 units and the other chord into segments that are 6 and 2 units. What is the diameter of the circle?

19. Two circles with different centers and three different straight lines lie in the same plane. What is the maximum number of possible points of intersections of all five objects?

20. Suppose there is a circle with diameter of 12 in. Inside this circle there are 1 billion points placed randomly. Draw a line through this circle so that exactly half of the points are on either side of the line AND so that the line does not intersect any of the points.

21. A person selling pencils packaged them in round, 1-inch radius bundles selling for a dollar. At the same rate, what would a round, 2-inch radius bundle be worth? Write an explanation of how you got your answer.

22. Gather several cylinders and a tape measure or calipers. A calculator will be useful for this activity. Measure the circumference and diameter for each of the cylinders. Compute $\dfrac{\text{circumference}}{\text{diameter}}$ for each item. Record the information in a table similar to the one shown.

circumference	diameter	$\dfrac{\text{circumference}}{\text{diameter}}$

Write an explanation of any similarities or differences you observe.

23. A kid is full after eating a round six-inch diameter pizza. On another day, with another kid who has the same eating capacity, the kids want to buy one pizza. What diameter should the pizza be so that when they are done they are both full and there are no left-overs? Write an explanation of how you got your answer.

24. If 450 grams of dough are used to make a pizza with a diameter of 40 cm, how many grams of dough are used to make a pizza with a diameter of 50 cm? (Assume the thickness of the pizzas remain constant). Write an explanation of how you got your answer.

25. Quadrilateral ABCD is a rhombus. Its diagonals are 12 and 20 units in length. Find the diameter of the circle inscribed in rhombus ABCD. Write an explanation of how you got your answer.

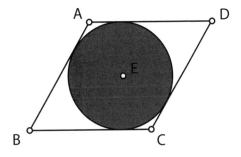

26. Suppose your car has 14-inch diameter tires in the front and 16-inch diameter tires in the rear. While it is parked, you mark the bottom of the front wheel and the bottom of the rear wheel with a piece of chalk. Then you drive off slowly. How far do you drive before both front and rear chalk marks are at the bottom again? Give your answer in feet. Write an explanation of how you got your answer.

27. Arrange 6 congruent circles of diameter d in the form of a triangle so there are 3 circles on each side (double counting the "vertex circles" for each side). Wrap a string around the figure ("triangle" with "rounded" corners). How long is the string? Write an explanation of how you got your answer.

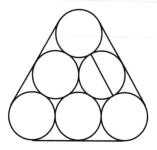

28. If the earth were reduced to the size of a soccer ball, would the earth or soccer ball be coarser? (The diameter of the earth is about 21,008,452 feet; Mount Everest is about 29,300 feet high; the Mariana Trench is about 35,640 feet deep.) Write an explanation of how you got your answer.

29. Suppose your car tires have a 24-inch diameter. You put on new tires that have a 25-inch diameter. This will cause your speedometer to produce an incorrect rate of speed. When your car reads 60 mph (miles per hour) with your new tires, what is your actual speed? (Assume travel is on a straight flat road.)

30. Given a circle, use three line segments (curved, straight, open, or closed) to subdivide the circle into eight sections. Write an explanation of how you got your answer.

31. Given a circle, use three line segments (curved, straight, open, or closed) to subdivide the circle into eight sections where each of the sections has the same area. Write an explanation of how you got your answer.

32. A large sphere is on a horizontal surface on a clear, sunny day and casts a shadow that is 10 m long when measured from where the sphere touches the surface. At the same instant in time, a meter stick, placed on the same horizontal surface and perpendicular to it, casts a 2 m long shadow. What is the radius of the sphere? For the sake of this problem, assume the sun's rays are parallel and that the meter stick is a line segment. Write an explanation of how you got your answer.

33. A running track has straight parallel sides and semicircular ends. It measures Y long as you go along the inside edge of the inside lane. The innermost lane is Lane 1. The next lane to it is Lane 2. Each lane is one meter wide. Assume that the finish line is at the center of one of the straight sides and perpendicular to that straight side of the track. The race we are discussing is a one-lap race that requires runners to stay in their respective lanes for the entire race, so a staggered start is necessary to compensate for the radii of the circles in the ends. How far ahead of the starting mark for Lane 1 should the starting mark for Lane 2 be placed so both runners cover the same distance as they make their lap? Write an explanation of how you got your answer.

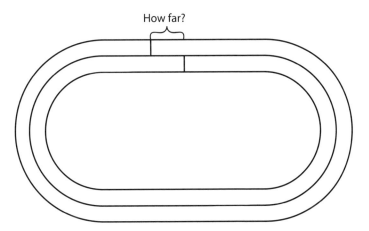

34. Draw a large scalene triangle. In that triangle, construct the three altitudes (perpendiculars drawn from a vertex to the opposite side of the triangle). Write your conclusions about the altitudes you created. Write an explanation of how you got your answer, or draw a sketch of your results.

35. Draw a large scalene triangle. In that triangle, construct the three angle bisectors. Write conclusions about these angle bisectors. Write an explanation of how you got your answer, or draw a sketch of your results.

36. Draw a large scalene triangle. In that triangle, construct the three medians (segments drawn from a vertex to the midpoint of the opposite side of the triangle). Write any conclusions about the medians you created. Write an explanation of how you got your answer or draw a sketch of your results.

37. Draw a large scalene triangle. In that triangle, construct the three medians (segments drawn from a vertex to the midpoint of the opposite side of the triangle). Measure the portion of each median that falls on either side of the point of concurrence. Write any conclusions about the ratio of those lengths. Write an explanation of how you got your answer or draw a sketch of your results.

38. Draw a large scalene triangle. In that triangle, construct the three midlines (perpendicular bisectors of each side of the triangle). Write any conclusions about the midlines you created. Write an explanation of how you got your answer or draw a sketch of your results.

39. Given a point, six equilateral triangles can be placed adjacent to each other so all space about that point is occupied. Since each angle of the equilateral triangle is 60°, the sum of all the angles about the point is 360°. Starting with any triangle, can six copies of it be arranged around a point as was done with the six equilateral triangles? Write an explanation of how you got your answer or draw a sketch of your result.

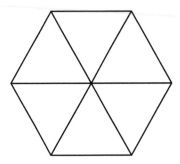

40. How can you arrange six toothpicks to form four congruent equilateral triangles? The side length of each triangle must equal the length of a whole toothpick. Write an explanation of how you got your answer or provide a sketch of it.

41. The following instructions will lead you to a construction of a 9-point circle, which is a historic geometric construction. While it can be done with compass and straightedge, it is much easier to do with a dynamic geometry program (Geometer's Sketchpad, Cabri, etc.). The 9-point circle passes through the base of each altitude, the midpoint of each side, and the midpoints of each segment joining a vertex to the point shared by the three altitudes. You will be asked to explain your construction, or provide a completed sketch of your work.

Draw a large scalene triangle ABC, locating the midpoints of each side D, E, and F. In that triangle, construct the three altitudes (perpendiculars drawn from a vertex to the opposite side of the triangle), naming them G, H, and J. Create segment AK with midpoint N, segment BK with midpoint L, and segment CK with midpoint M. Create segments DM, FL, and EN, which are concurrent (intersect at a common point) at point P. P is the center of the 9-point circle that passes through points G, L, E, H, M, J, F, N, and D. Write an explanation of your construction or draw a sketch of your results.

42.   Using nine toothpicks, how can you form three congruent (same size and shape) squares, while having each side be exactly one toothpick length long? Write an explanation of your solution or draw a sketch of it.

43.   What would you get if you use 12 toothpicks to make a shape comprised of six smaller congruent shapes? The toothpicks may not be bent or broken. A toothpick is one unit and fractional units may not serve as a side length. Sketch your result.

44. You are given 24 toothpicks. They may not be bent or broken. As you complete the following tasks, partial lengths of toothpicks are not to be used.

How many squares can be made using 6-toothpick lengths per side? ___

How many squares can be made using 5-toothpick lengths per side? ___

How many squares can be made using 4-toothpick lengths per side? ___

How many squares can be made using 3-toothpick lengths per side? ___

How many squares can be made using 2-toothpick lengths per side? ___

How many squares can be made using 1-toothpick length per side? ___

Note: you may not be able to use all of the toothpicks each time and the squares produced may not all be the same size. For example, using three-toothpick lengths per side, you could make three squares:

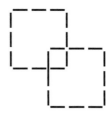

45. Cut a scalene triangle out of a piece of paper (this activity could be done using a dynamic software product like Geometer's Sketchpad or Cabri). Label the vertices of the triangle A, B, and C. Tear each vertex off the triangle. Place vertex A on a smooth flat surface. Place vertex B so it is adjacent to vertex A (share a common endpoint and side). Place vertex C so it is adjacent to either vertex A or vertex B. Write a description of the edges that are not shared with the vertex that is between the other two, or draw a sketch of your results.

46.   I am putting carpet on the floor of a 12 feet by 12 feet room. I have a 16 feet by 9 feet piece of carpet that has no pattern and is uniform in color. I am able to make carpet seams any way I elect to do so, and am able to attach it to tack strips on the edges of the room with no excess carpet needed. What is the fewest number of pieces I can cut the 16 by 9 piece to make a 12 by 12 piece? Describe how you would cut the 16 by 9 piece to accomplish the task or draw a sketch of your results.

47.   Construct a circle with center G. Mark points M, N, and H on the circle. Connect M and N with G. Connect M and N with H. Measure angles MGN and MHN. Move the points on the circle. Change the length of the radius of the circle. Describe the relation between angles MGN and MHN in writing, or draw a sketch of your results.

48. How do you subdivide a line segment into three congruent segments via construction? Write an explanation of how you got your answer.

49. Start with four pieces of stick spaghetti. Divide each spaghetti stick into three parts. Keep the sets together. Do this before reading on.

You were to divide each of the three pieces of spaghetti before reading this. If you have not done that, please do it now. Which of the four sets of three pieces of spaghetti can be used to create a triangle? The full piece of each part must be used to form a side of the triangle and the ends of the pieces must meet at a vertex of the triangle. What is the probability of getting a triangle from the sets you created? Try this with a group of people and see if your results change. What generalization can you make about the requirements for forming a triangle from the activity you have just completed? Write an explanation of how you got your answer or draw a sketch of your results.

50. Make a tool like the one shown. The line segments are strings emanating from a single point. The piece with the circular hole in it is made from cardboard. Make similar pieces with different holes in them: square, equilateral triangle, isosceles trapezoid, and parallelogram. Predict what the projection of each hole will be on a surface perpendicular to the plane of the hole. Use the tool to check your prediction. Could this activity be done using materials other than the apparatus shown? Write an explanation of your results.

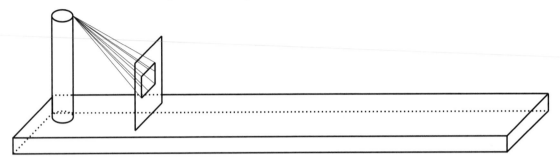

51. Make a figure that consists of two squares and four triangles from toothpicks without breaking or bending any of the toothpicks. Not all shapes will have a full toothpick length as a side. Write an explanation of how you got your answer or draw a sketch of your solution.

52. Using only 12 straight, congruent line segments, describe a figure that is comprised of six congruent regions. Write an explanation of how you got your answer. Solve this one more than one way and receive a bonus point!

53. Triangles can be shown to be congruent by a variety of methods. Which of the following properties can always be used to create a triangle congruent to a given triangle: SSA, AAA, SSS, ASA, SAS, SAA? Make a construction to demonstrate any property that will not always yield a triangle that is congruent to a given triangle. Write an explanation of how you got your answer.

————————————————————————

54. Two horizontal, parallel lines (AB and CD) are cut by transversals EF and GH. What is the sum of the measures of angles ∠BGP, ∠GPM, and ∠PMD?

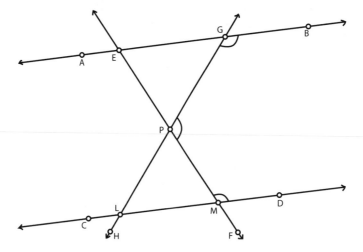

55. In ΔABC, the bisectors of ∠ABC and ∠ACB intersect at point D. What is the measure of ∠BAC if ∠BDC measures 140°? Write an explanation of how you got your answer.

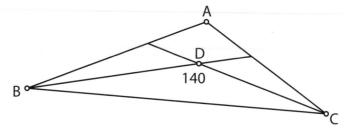

56. Draw a circle with a 10 cm diameter. Construct an equilateral triangle such that one its sides is a diameter of the circle. What is the area of the region of the semi-circle that is outside the triangle (shaded in the figure)? Write an explanation of how you got your answer, or draw a sketch of your results.

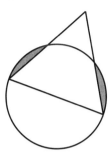

57. In the below construction, $\overleftrightarrow{AB}$ is parallel to $\overleftrightarrow{CD}$. The measure of ∠ACB is 90°. $\overline{AC} \cong \overline{BC}$ and $\overline{AB} \cong \overline{BD}$. Find the measure of ∠CBD.

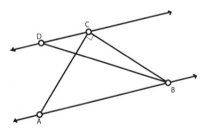

58. In triangle ABC with right angle C, $\overline{CD}$ is perpendicular to $\overline{AB}$. If E is the midpoint of $\overline{DB}$, show that the measure of angle ACE > the measure of angle AEC. Write an explanation of how you got your answer.

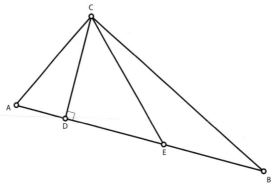

59. Think about different possible scalene triangles in which all angle measures are whole numbers (for example: 11°, 27°, and 142° sum to 180°). Find the difference between the largest possible sum of the two largest angles and smallest possible sum of the two largest angles. Write an explanation of how you got your answer.

60. In ΔABC, the measure of ∠A is 30º, and the measure of ∠B is 45º. If M is the midpoint of $\overline{AC}$, find the measure of ∠MBC. Write an explanation of your answer.

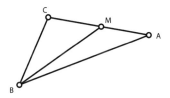

61. You are given ΔABC with ∠ABC = 45º. You have a segment connecting A to a point D on $\overline{BC}$, such that 2 $\overline{BD}$ = $\overline{CD}$ and you know that the measure of ∠DAB = 15º. Find the measure of ∠ACB.

62. What is the area of each possible triangle with a perimeter of 8 units when side lengths are required to be integers? Write an explanation of how you got your answer or draw a sketch, labeling the appropriate lengths.

63. Given a circle O with a diameter of 10 cm and an equilateral triangle ABC with one of its sides being the diameter, what is the area of the region of the circle created by the sides of the triangle (not the diameter) and the circle?

64. Draw a large circle on a piece of paper. Divide that circle into eight congruent,
     pie-shaped pieces and put them together as shown.

 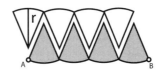

Notice that the figure on the right appears to be a parallelogram with "rounded
sections" on the long sides. If those "rounded sections" between points A and B
were straightened out, what is the measure of segment AB in terms of the radius,
(r) and π? The height of the "parallelogram" would be the radius (r). What is the
area of the "parallelogram" in terms of π and r? Write an explanation of how you
got your answer.

65.   A regular hexagon is inscribed (vertices lie on the circle) in a circle.
      a. What percent of the area of the circle is overlapped by the area of the
         inscribed regular hexagon?
      b. If the radius of the circle is tripled and a regular hexagon is inscribed in the
         new circle, what percent of the area of the circle is overlapped by the area
         of the inscribed regular hexagon?

66.   Find the area of an equilateral triangle inscribed in a circle whose circumference
      is 3π. Write an explanation of how you got your answer.

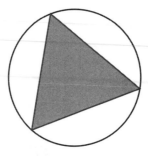

67.   Triangle DEF is constructed by the midpoints of the sides of triangle ABC.
          a. How do the areas of triangle ABC and triangle DEF compare?
          b. How do the perimeters of triangle ABC and triangle DEF compare?

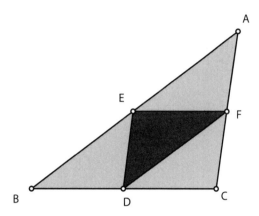

68.   Square ABCD is comprised of one inner square and four shaded, congruent
       rectangles. If each shaded rectangle has a perimeter of 20 units, what is the area
       of square ABCD?

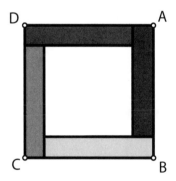

69. The diagonals of a rhombus have lengths of 12 m and 16 m. What is the difference in the values of the perimeter and area of the rhombus?

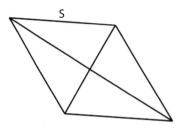

70. My dog Fido is chained to the outside corner of my rectangular house. His chain is 5 meters long. What is the size of the area the dog can roam while still being attached to the chain?

71. Quadrilateral ABCD is a trapezoid where side AD is congruent to side BC. If the altitude of the trapezoid (segment AE) is 12 units and diagonal AC is 18 units in length, what is the area of trapezoid ABCD?

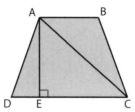

72. A square window is one-yard high and one-yard wide. How can the area of the window be cut in half while still measuring one-yard high and one-yard wide? Write an explanation of how you got your answer or draw a sketch of your results.

1 yard

73. Each edge of the cube measures 5 units in length. Points B and D are each
     midpoints of an edge of the cube. What is the perimeter of quadrilateral ABCD?
     Write an explanation of how you got your answer.

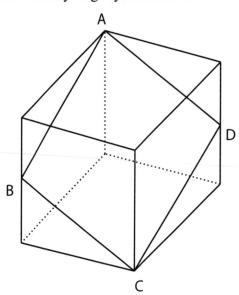

74.   A trapezoid is inscribed in a circle with a radius of 3 units. One base of the trapezoid is the diameter of the circle. The other base has a length of 3 units. What is the perimeter of the trapezoid? Write an explanation of how you got your answer.

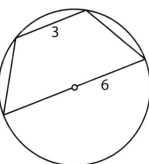

75.   In this regular hexagon, $\overline{AD}$ and $\overline{BD}$ are 4 units long. $\overline{CD}$ is twice as long as $\overline{AD}$. What is the perimeter of the hexagon?

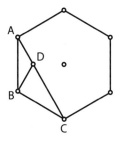

76.   Quadrilateral ABCD is a square with side lengths of 20 cm. The distance from
      point N to point M is 16 cm. If each of the shaded regions represents equal
      isosceles triangles, what is the area of the non-shaded region inside the square?

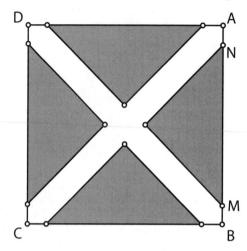

77.   The side lengths of an isosceles triangle are 5a + 20, a + 196, and 3a + 76
      respectively. If "a" represents a rational number, what is the greatest possible
      perimeter of this isosceles triangle?

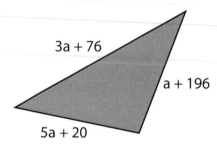

78. The Mitsubishi logo is made up of 3 congruent rhombi, each of which is made up of 2 congruent equilateral triangles. The entire logo is made up of parts of a large equilateral triangle, the side length of which is 3 times the side length of one of the smaller equilateral triangles that make up any rhombus. Using "a" for the side length of the big triangle, what is the area of the logo? Write to explain how you got your answer.

79. Draw a circle with a 10 cm diameter. Construct an equilateral triangle such that one its sides is a diameter of the circle. What is the area of the region of the circle that is inside the triangle (shaded in the figure)? Write an explanation of how you got your answer or draw a sketch of your results.

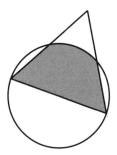

80. A rhombus has diagonals of lengths 12 and 16 units. What is the perimeter and area of the rhombus? Write an explanation of how you got your answer.

81. You have a regular hexagonal fenced area in your backyard. Rover, your dog, is tied with a 12-meter chain at one of the vertices of the regular hexagon. The perimeter of the fence is 78 meters. Your veterinarian recommends that Rover have at least 150 square meters of roaming room. Does Rover have enough roaming room? How much roaming room does Rover have? You must answer both questions. Write an explanation of how you got your answer.

82.   What is the ratio of the area of the shaded square compared to the area of the large square? Write an explanation of how you got your answer.

83.   What is the area of the largest square that can be cut from a regular octagonal stop sign that has sides measuring 6 inches in length?

84. The minute and hour hands of a clock have measurements of 5 inches and 3 inches, respectively. Over a 6.5-hour period, how much total surface area, in square inches, on the face of the clock do the hands pass over?

85. Triangles ABC and MNO are congruent, isosceles, right triangles. Triangle ABC contains the inscribed square BDEF (D, E, and F are midpoints of their respective sides) and triangle MNO contains the inscribed square PQRS. If the area of square BDEF is 441 square units, find the area of square PQRS.

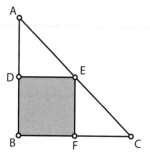
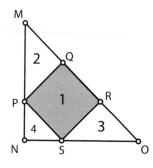

86. A rectangle is divided into four sub rectangles with areas 4, 7, 15, and A square meters. Find the exact area of sub rectangle A. Draw a picture and explain your work.

87. Imagine you move a heavy, flat-bottomed box by placing it on a bunch of rollers that have a 14-inch diameter. The non-stationary rollers are on a smooth horizontal surface. In relation to the ground, how far will the box move when each roller makes exactly one complete revolution? Write an explanation of how you got your answer.

88. What is the length of the side of a square inscribed in a circle that has a circumference of 100 units? Write an explanation of how you got your answer.

89. Suppose a square and a circle have the same area. If the length of the diagonal of the square is 3 cm, what is the radius of the circle? Write an explanation of how you got your answer.

90. Suppose you set up a model to show the relation of the distance between the moon and the earth. One person holds a ball representing the earth and another holds a ball representing the moon. How far apart should the two people stand in the model to represent the distance between the earth and the moon? Write an explanation of how you got your answer.

91. While attending the circus, you see an amazing site: Theodore the Fantastic Frog. Theodore sits on a stand with his mouth 5 feet 6 inches above the ground. People walk past Theodore one-by-one. When standing directly in front of the frog, each person is exactly one foot from Theodore. The amazing part occurs when a person passes in front of Theodore. He sticks out his tongue and touches their nose. If the tallest person's nose that Theodore can touch has a nose that is exactly 6 feet 4 inches off the ground, answer the following questions:

   a. What would be the height of the nose of the shortest person that Theodore could lick?

   b. What is the maximum distance that Theodore can stick out his tongue?

92. Each side of △ABC is 75 units in length. Point D is the foot of the altitude drawn from A to side $\overline{BC}$. Point E is the midpoint of segment $\overline{AD}$. What is the length of $\overline{BE}$?

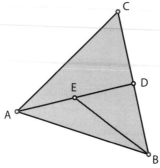

93. A rectangular prism (box) has a length of 21 m, a width of 16 m, and a height of 12 m. Find the length of the greatest possible straight line segment that can be contained in this box. Write an explanation of how you got your answer. Try solving this problem more than one way.

94. Checkers and chessboards are an 8 by 8 array of squares. In chess, the knight always follows an "L" pattern as it moves – two squares in one direction and one square perpendicular to the original path (or one square followed by two squares on the perpendicular path). Assuming the knight is at its starting square (on a side, second square from the corner), that its position is always at the center of a square, and that the squares are two inches on a side, what is the maximum distance the knight can go in three moves (assuming it is not captured and there are no obstructions)? What is the minimum distance after three moves? Write an explanation of your result.

95.   Triangles ABC and ADE are equilateral triangles. Determine the length of $\overline{EF}$.

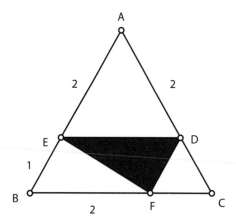

96.   You have a cylinder with an outside diameter of 3 cm and a height of 15 cm. Ten turns of wire are helically wrapped around the cylinder so the respective ends are at the top and bottom of a height segment drawn on the outside of the cylinder. How long is the wire to the nearest centimeter? Write an explanation of how you got your answer.

97.   David has built a time machine with three sprockets arranged in an equilateral triangle. The radius of each of the three sprockets is 10 cm and the distance between the centers of each sprocket is 1 m. David must connect the three sprockets with a chain. How long must the chain be? Write an explanation of how you got your answer.

98.   Two by fours (2 x 4) are a common wooden building material used in construction. Unfortunately, the name does not accurately describe the dimensions of the piece of lumber. The actual dimensions are 1.5 by 3.5 inches. When building a wall, these boards are placed so that the centers of the 1.5 inch sides are 16 inches apart (or maybe 24 inches apart). If a wall contains 5 of these 2 x 4 boards, how long in feet and inches is the wall? Write an explanation of how you got your answer, or draw a sketch of your results.

99. Arrange four points on a plane so the distance between any two points is one of two possible lengths. For example, one solution would be to have the four points be vertices of a square. The side lengths of the square would be one length. The diagonals would be the second length. There are at least four other figures that will satisfy these conditions. Write an explanation of how you got your answer, or draw a sketch.

100. Two parallel poles (6 inch diameter and 18 inch diameter) are tangent to each other. What is the minimum distance around both poles as they are configured? Visualize wrapping a band around them to hold them together. Write an explanation of how you got your answer.

101. A mirror, a marble, a tape measure, and level ground can be used to measure the height of a tall object. Use the marble to assure the mirror is level. Stand away from the mirror and then move so the top of the object can be seen in the mirror. Measure the distance from your eyes to the ground (EY), the distance from the point beneath your eyes to the top of the object in the mirror (YM), and the distance from the top of the object in the mirror to a point beneath the top of the object (MB). Similar triangles have been established and the ratio of the distances will equal the ratio of the respective heights. Solve the proportion for the unknown height (BT). (Professor Kenneth Kidd of the University of Florida developed this idea.) Write an explanation of how you got your answer.

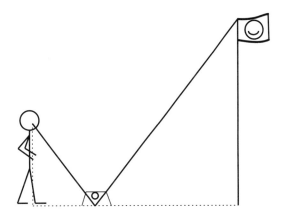

VOLUME & SURFACE AREA

102. How can you cut a square layer cake that has been frosted on top and all sides (but not the bottom) into 16 pieces so that each piece will contain the same amount of frosting and the same volume of cake? Write an explanation of how you got your answer, or draw a sketch of your results.

103. A wedding cake is made from three 8 cm high circular tiers. The tiers have diameters of 60 cm, 48 cm, and 36 cm respectively. The cake must be frosted with white icing. There will be no frosting between layers or on the bottom surface on which the cake sits. What is the surface area to be covered by frosting?

104. A large cube is painted on all 6 faces. It is then cut into smaller cubes so the number of cubes with no paint on any face is 8 times the number of smaller cubes with paint on exactly 3 faces. How many little cubes are made from the large cube? Write an explanation of how you got your answer.

105. A uniform, right, cylindrical pipe is being lowered into a water tank that is a right rectangular prism. The height of the tank is 8 meters and the dimensions of the base are 20 meters by 10 meters. The pipe is being lowered so that it will stand up in the tank (the base of the cylinder is parallel to the bottom of the tank). After the pipe is lowered into the water tank, exactly half of the pipe is submerged, which caused the water level in the tank to rise 0.65 cm. If the pipe has a radius of 1 meter and is made of steel, find the volume of the pipe. Write an explanation of how you got your answer.

106. You have three cubes whose edges are 2, 6, and 8 meters long, respectively. What is the minimum possible surface area when the three cubes are glued together at their faces? Write an explanation of how you got your answer.

107. A company decides to alter a soda can by increasing the height by 30 percent. The can is a right circular cylinder. If the company does not want to increase the volume of the can, by what percentage must the radius be increased or decreased to keep the volume the same? You must indicate whether the radius will be increased or decreased as well as by what percentage. Write an explanation of how you got your answer.

108. A square piece of tin is made into an open box by cutting a square of side length X from each corner and then turning up the sides. The volume of the box is C cubic inches. Find the side length, "S", of the original square in terms of X and C. Assume the edges of the turned up sections meet exactly with no overlap. Write an explanation of how you got your answer or draw a sketch of your results.

109. One glass is half-full of juice. A second glass, twice the size of the first glass, is one-quarter full of juice. Water is added to both glasses until they are full. The contents of the two full glasses are dumped into a third container (large enough to hold them both). What part of the mixture in the third container is juice? Write an explanation of how you got your answer.

110. In triangle ABC, segment AC = 6 units and segment BC = 8 units. Angles ACB and BED are both right angles. If segment DE = 4 units, what is the length of segment BD? Write an explanation of how you got your answer or draw a sketch of your results.

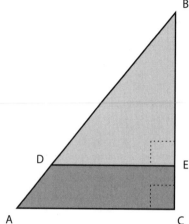

111. Imagine a canyon that is spanned by a bridge that is exactly one mile long. The bridge has no expansion joints in it, so when it heats, it bows up. One hot day, the bridge lengthened by two feet to a total length of one mile plus two feet. Approximately how high above its original unheated position is the center of the expanded bridge? Write an explanation of how you got your answer or draw a sketch of your results.

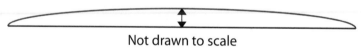

Not drawn to scale

112. A circle of radius (r) is inscribed in a right triangle with hypotenuse (h). What is the ratio of the area of the circle to the area of the right triangle? Write an explanation of how you got your answer.

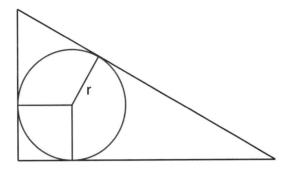

113. Find the radius of the incircle (the largest circle contained inside the triangle) of triangle ABC with side lengths of 7, 24, and 25 units. Write an explanation of how you got your answer.

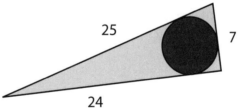

114. The hypotenuse of a right triangle is 6 units. The perimeter of the triangle is 14 units. Find the area of the right triangle. Write an explanation of how you got your answer.

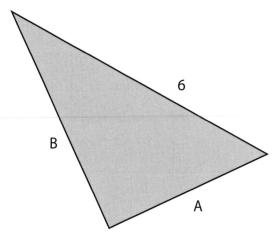

115. For this problem, assume the ground is horizontal and the wall is vertical. A 25 foot ladder is placed against the vertical wall of a building. The foot of the ladder is 7 feet from the base of the wall. If the top of the ladder slides down 4 feet on the wall, how far out will the base of the ladder slide?

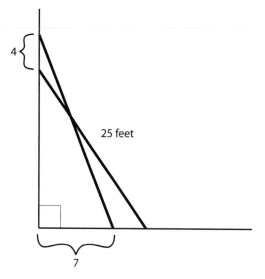

116. In right triangle ABC, with C as the right angle, it is known that $\overline{AD} = \overline{DE} = \overline{BE}$ and that D and E are points on hypotenuse $\overline{AB}$. It is also known that $\overline{CD} = 7$ units and $\overline{CE} = 9$ units. What is the length of $\overline{AB}$?

117. When the pieces below are arranged one way, it appears as though the area is 32 square units and 32.5 square units the other way. We know that cannot be if the four pieces used are the same size and shape when they are used, which they are. Explain in writing what is wrong.

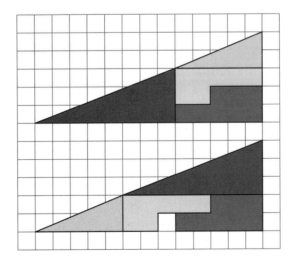

118. A tracker followed a bear three miles south, three miles west, and then three miles north. After the nine-mile trek, the tracker was back at the initial starting point. What color was the bear that was being tracked? Write an explanation of how you got your answer.

119. How can these five pieces be put together to form a square? You will find it helpful to cut these pieces out of paper or cardboard.

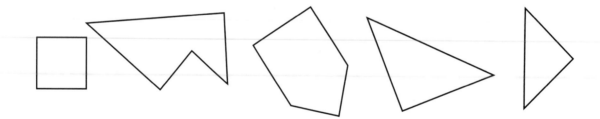

120. Your task is to plant ten trees so they are in five rows and there are four trees per row. Draw a sketch to show your solution.

121. You and a friend are about to play a game for which you need a round table and a large number of identical round coasters or napkins in two different colors. The players will take turns placing one coaster at a time on the tabletop. The coasters may touch, but they may not overlap at any time. The player who is able to put the last coaster on the table has won the game. You have thought about this game for some time and have a strategy that guarantees a win. Write an explanation of your winning plan.

122. A clock runs backwards (hands move counterclockwise), but at the proper rate. If the clock is initially set to the correct time, how many times in one complete day will it show the correct time? Write an explanation of how you got your answer.

123. One figure is missing from the set of 12. There is a pattern defined by the 11 figures that are present. Use that information to provide the missing piece. Write an explanation of how you got your answer or draw a sketch of your results.

124. A cable, 16 meters in length, hangs between two pillars that are both 15 meters high. The ends of the cable are attached to the tops of the pillars. At its lowest point, the cable hangs 7 meters above the ground. How far apart are the two pillars? Write an explanation of how you got your answer.

125. Remove two toothpicks from the given arrangement so that the new arrangement will consist of only four congruent squares. Each side length of any square equals the length of the whole toothpick. Write an explanation or draw a picture that shows how you got your answer. Show at least two different solutions.

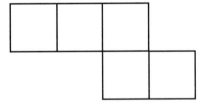

126. A rhombus is formed by two congruent equilateral triangles sharing a common side. The midpoints of each of the sides of the equilateral triangles are connected, creating eight smaller congruent equilaterals. Use toothpicks to form each side of the small triangles and then remove four toothpicks from this figure, leaving exactly four triangles. Do this at least two different ways. Write an explanation or draw a picture that shows how you got your answer.

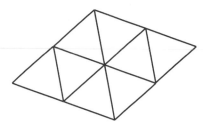

127. Square ABCD is divided and shaded as shown below. The red square is one-fourth the area of square ABCD. If the pattern continued forever and ever, what percentage of the original square would be shaded?

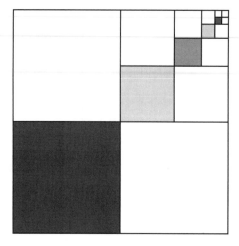

128. A teacher places three students in a line on three chairs, in such a way that Kid C can see both Kid A and Kid B. Kid B can see only Kid A. Kid A can see none of the other kids. The teacher shows all three kids 5 hats, 2 of which are black and 3 of which are white. After this, the kids are blindfolded while the teacher places one hat on each of their heads. After the hats are in place, the blindfolds are removed. The teacher tells the kids that if any one of them is able to determine the color of the hat they are wearing, they will get homework passes for five assignments. None of the kids can see the hat on their head. The kids get the homework pass because Kid A figures it out. How did Kid A figure out what he was wearing? Why didn't Kid B or C correctly identify their own hat?

129. How many squares are on an 8 by 8 checkerboard? Write an explanation of how you got your answer.

130. How are the following numbers related and what does each represent?
9.86965, 0.7854, 6.2832, 6141.3

131. Each of the figures below is made up of five congruent squares. All 30 of the squares are congruent. List at least five questions you could ask about these figures. Write the answer to each of your questions.

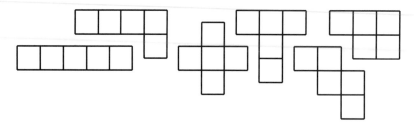

132. Suppose you wanted to purchase a piece of property that is bounded by two segments that run exactly east and west, and two other bounding segments that run exactly north and south. You also want the east to west segments to be the exact same length. Where would the center of the desired property have to be located? Write an explanation of how you got your answer.

SOLUTIONS

1. SOLUTION:

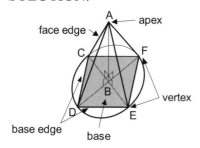

Since the pyramid is isosceles, all of the base edges ($\overline{CD}$, $\overline{DE}$, $\overline{EF}$, $\overline{CF}$) must be congruent and all of the face edges ($\overline{AC}$, $\overline{AD}$, $\overline{AE}$, $\overline{AF}$) must be congruent. Since pyramid bases are convex, the base must be a regular polygon (CDEF is a square). The altitude ($\overline{AB}$) is perpendicular to the base, passing through the apex (point A). Thus, right triangles (ABC, ABD, ABE, ABF) are generated composed of the altitude, the face edge, and the segment joining the vertices of the base with the point at the foot of the altitude. These right triangles must be congruent since they each have a congruent hypotenuse (face edge) and leg (altitude). But that says the remaining leg (from the point at the base of the altitude to each base vertex – $\overline{BC}$, $\overline{BD}$, $\overline{BE}$, $\overline{BF}$)) of each triangle is congruent. These remaining legs form radii of a circle that circumscribes the base. It should be noted that this argument will be true for any isosceles pyramid because its base will be a regular polygon (all sides and angles are congruent).

6 possible points
1 point (content): Realize base edges must be congruent.
1 point (content): Realize the base must be a regular polygon.
1 point (content): Realize triangles formed by altitude and edges are congruent.
1 point (content): Realize remaining legs are congruent.
1 point (content): Realize base legs are radii of circumscribing circle.
1 point (clarity): The explanation is clearly written.

2. ANSWER: $\dfrac{h}{12}$ (h is the height of the cone) units, or 0.08333h units.

SOLUTION: The catch is that the formulas use r and h as variables. Be careful here not to divide out the h and H in the following solution.

The volume of our cone is $\dfrac{\pi r^2 h}{3}$.

The volume of a cylinder is $\pi r^2 h$, which becomes $\pi 4 r^2 H$ for our cylinder, where H is the height.

Setting the equations equal to each other makes $\dfrac{\pi r^2 h}{3} = \pi 4 r^2 H$.

Dividing out π gives $\dfrac{r^2 h}{3} = 4 r^2 H$.

Divide again by $4r^2$ to solve for H.

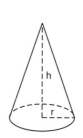
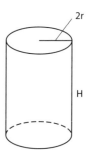

This gives $\frac{h}{12}$ = H, where h is the height of the cone and H is the height of the cylinder.

RUBRIC
5 possible points
1 point (content): Realize the express both radii in terms of r.
1 point (content): Realize the heights will be different (h and H).
1 point (content): Realize the need to set the two formulas equal to each other.
1 point (content): The algebra is correct.
1 point (clarity): The explanation is clearly written.

3.　ANSWER: 24 edges.

SOLUTION: Count the edges.
5 possible points
1 point (content): Construct the tetrahedron correctly.
1 point (content): Construct the tetrahedron at each of the 8 vertices.
1 point (content): Realize each tetrahedron generates 3 edges.
1 point (content): Count the total of 24 edges from the 8 tetrahedrons.
1 point (clarity): The explanation is clearly written.

4.　ANSWER: 5 circles. Sum of the diameters is 47 cm.

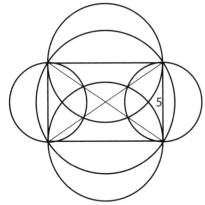

SOLUTION: The four vertices determine six possible diameters: the four sides and two diagonals, but the diagonals are diameters of the same circle. Therefore, there are five circles. The two small circles on the short sides of the rectangle of have diameters of 5 cm, the two circles on the long sides of the rectangle have diameters of 12 cm, and the fifth circle for the diagonals of the rectangle has a diameter of 13 cm (use the Pythagorean theorem with 5 and 12 being the sides of a right triangle. The hypotenuse, 13, would be the diagonal).
$5 + 5 + 12 + 12 + 13 = 47$

4 possible points
1 point (content): Use the Pythagorean theorem to find the diagonal length.
1 point (content): Realize each side will be a diameter of a different circle.
1 point (content): Realize the diagonals of the rectangle will generate the same circle.
1 point (clarity): The explanation is clearly written.

5. **ANSWER:** As the number of sides increases, the area of the polygon approaches the area of the circle.

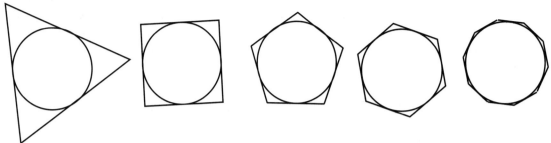

Observation shows that as the number of sides of the regular polygon increases, the regular polygon gets closer to looking like a circle, meaning that the area of the regular polygon gets closer to the area of the circle as the number of sides increases.

3 possible points
1 point (content): Figures drawn correctly.
1 point (content): Pattern discovered.
1 point (clarity): The explanation is clearly written.

6. **SOLUTION:** A regular polygon can be inscribed in a circle. The interior angles of this polygon are 156°. Construct two adjacent triangles with a common vertex at the center of the circle. The other common vertex (on the common side) of the two triangles will be the center point of a 156° angle. That common side bisects that 156° angle. Thus the base angles of each triangle is 78°, making the central angle 24°. $\frac{360}{24} = 15$.

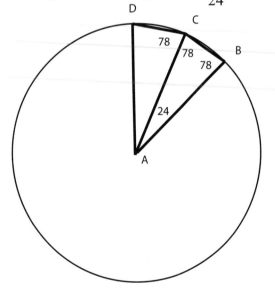

Solution 2: Use the formula for the sum of the interior angles of a convex polygon.
1. (n-2)180 = sum = 156n
180n - 360 = 156n
-360 = -24n
15 = n

7.   ANSWER: 12 units.

SOLUTION: Since ∠DCF + ∠FCB = 90°, ∠DCF≅ ∠BCE. ∠FDC ≅ ∠EBC, since both are right angles. $\overline{CD}$ ≅ $\overline{CB}$, since both segments are sides of a square. By ASA, ΔCDF ≅ ΔCBE. Therefore, $\overline{CE}$ ≅ $\overline{CF}$. This shows that ΔCEF is isosceles. Its area is then $\dfrac{\overline{CE}^2}{2}$ = 200, so $\overline{CE}^2$ = 400 square units.

By the Pythagorean theorem, $(\overline{CB})^2 + (\overline{BE})^2 = (\overline{CE})^2$ [$(\overline{CB})^2$ = area of square].

So, $256 + (\overline{BE})^2 = 400$, or $(\overline{BE})^2 = 144$, or $\overline{BE}$ = 12 units.

6 possible points
1 point (content): Realize ∠DCF is congruent to ∠BCE.
1 point (content): Realize ΔCDF is congruent to ΔCBE.
1 point (content): Realize segment CE is congruent to CF.
1 point (content): Realize ΔCEF is isosceles.
1 point (content): The arithmetic is correct.
1 point (clarity): The explanation is clearly written.

8.   ANSWER: 27 sides.

SOLUTION: If the polygon has n sides, then it has n vertices. Also n – 3 diagonals connect each vertex to every other vertex other than itself and the two vertices adjacent to it.

Therefore, the polygon has $\dfrac{n(n-3)}{2}$ = 324 diagonals.

Simplifying, n(n – 3) = 648
And, $n^2 – 3n – 648 = 0$
Solving, n = 27 or –24
Since you cannot have a negative number of sides for a polygon, the answer is 27.
    ALTERNATE SOLUTION:

# of sides	3	4	5	6	7	8	. . .	26	27
# of diagonals	0	2	5	9	14	20		299	324
difference between # diagonals and the preceding # diagonals		2	3	4	5	6		24	25
difference between difference between diagonals and preceding one			1	1	1	1		1	1

Use finite differences. Second difference is constant at 1. First difference increases by one each time.

4 possible points
1 point (content): Realize there is a pattern .
1 point (content): Correctly set up the algebraic equation, solve by <u>Factoring</u> or <u>Quadratic Formula</u>.
1 point (content): Determine 27 sides.
1 point (clarity): The explanation is clearly written.

9.   ANSWER: $\frac{51}{64}$ of the original triangle's area is shaded.

SOLUTION: The first round of line segments drawn divides the large triangle into 4 congruent smaller triangles. The second round of segment construction divides only one of these smaller triangles into further 4 smaller congruent triangles. And again this is repeated. Now the upright triangles are shaded. Three triangles created by the first set of midpoints are shaded covering $\frac{3}{4}$ of the original triangle's area. Three smallest triangles are shaded covering $\frac{3}{64}$ (those three small triangles are really $\frac{1}{4}$ of $\frac{1}{4}$ of $\frac{1}{4}$) of the original triangle's area. So $\frac{3}{4} + \frac{3}{64} = \frac{51}{64}$ of the original triangle's area is shaded.

5 possible points
1 point (content): Realize three different sets of midpoints are needed.
1 point (content): Realize the relation between the triangle sizes.
1 point (content): Realize that the largest shaded triangle is 16 times the smallest.
1 point (content): Realize that the medium shaded triangle is 4 times the smallest.
1 point (clarity): The explanation is clearly written.
BONUS: Realize this process is the same for any triangle.

10.   ANSWER: $\frac{17}{42}$ or about 0.40 or 40%.

SOLUTION: You must use segments such that a<b<c, a+b>c, a+c>b, and c+b>a. The number of triples is $_9C_3$ (combination of 9 things taken three at a time) or 84 such that a<b<c. The triples satisfying the other inequalities are:
(2,3,4), (2,4,5), (2,5,6), (2,6,7), (2,7,8), (2,8,9), (3,4,5), (3,4,6), (3,5,6), (3,5,7), (3,6,7), (3,6,8), (3,7,8), (3,7,9), (3,8,9), (4,5,6), (4,5,7), (4,5,8), (4,6,7), (4,6,8), (4,6,9), (4,7,8), (4,7,9), (4,8,9), (5,6,7), (5,6,8), (5,6,9), (5,7,8), (5,7,9), (5,8,9), (6,7,8), (6,7,9), (6,8,9), and (7,8,9) which is 34 triples out of 84.
$\frac{34}{84} = \frac{17}{42}$ or about 0.40 or 40%

11.   ANSWER: 4 to 1.

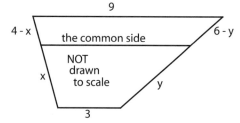

SOLUTION: Label the big part of the 6 unit nonparallel side as y and the small part of that same side as (6 - y). Similarly, label the big part of the 4 unit side as x and the small part as (4 - x). The one side is shared by both trapezoids. The perimeter of the bottom internal trapezoid is x + y + 3 + the common side, and the perimeter of the top internal trapezoid is (6 - y) + 9 + (4 - x) + the common side. These perimeters are equal. Subtract the common side from both sides and you have x + y + 3 = 19 − x − y; 2x + 2y = 16; x + y = 8. This is the sum of the nonparallel sides of the bottom trapezoid. The sum of the nonparallel sides of the top trapezoid is (6 - y) + (4 - x) or 10 - (x + y), but (x + y) = 8 and you have 10 − 8 = 2.
The ratio of the sum of the sides is 8:2, or 4:1.

This ratio is the same as the ratio into which each nonparallel side is divided. Note: $\frac{y}{6} = \frac{x}{4}$,

so $\frac{y}{x} = \frac{6}{4}$. x + y = 8, or y = x - 8. So $\frac{8-x}{x} = \frac{6}{4}$, and 32 - 4x = 6x, or x = $\frac{16}{5}$. Then $\frac{x}{4-x} =$

$$\frac{\frac{16}{5}}{4-\frac{16}{5}} = \frac{\frac{16}{5}}{\frac{4}{5}} = \frac{16}{4} = \frac{4}{1}.$$

4 possible points
1 point (content): Realize that the two smaller trapezoids share the common side.
1 point (content): Realize that the ratio of the sum of the sides is 4:1.
1 point (content): Formulas and computations used correctly.
1 point (clarity): The explanation is clearly written.

12.   ANSWER: 1 is false. 2 & 3 are true.

SOLUTION: When 3 altitudes, medians, and angle bisectors all lie entirely within the triangle (which they will except for obtuse or right triangles) where A, B, and C are the verticies of the triangle with interior points A', B', and C' on respective opposite sides, we have to look at $\overline{AA'}$ + $\overline{BB'}$ + $\overline{CC'}$. Since the sum of any 2 sides of a triangle is greater than the third side, (1) $\overline{AA'}$ + $\overline{A'B}$ > $\overline{AB}$ and (2) $\overline{AA'}$ + $\overline{A'C}$ > $\overline{AC}$. Adding (1) and (2) gives (3) 2$\overline{AA'}$ + $\overline{BC}$ > $\overline{AB}$ + $\overline{AC}$. (Remember, $\overline{A'B}$ + $\overline{A'C}$ = $\overline{AC}$.) Similarly, (4) 2$\overline{BB'}$ + $\overline{AC}$ > $\overline{BC}$ + $\overline{AB}$ and (5) 2$\overline{CC'}$ + $\overline{AB}$ > $\overline{AC}$ + $\overline{BC}$. Adding (3), (4), and (5) gives (6) 2($\overline{AA'}$ + $\overline{BB'}$ + $\overline{CC'}$) > $\overline{AB}$ + $\overline{BC}$ + $\overline{AC}$. So, assertions 2 and 3 are true and 1 is true for acute triangles.

As a counter example to assertion 1, consider an isosceles triangle with base "b" and base angles A. As A tends to zero, each altitude tends to zero, while the perimeter tends to 2b. An angle sufficiently close to zero refutes assertion 1.

5 possible points
1 point (content): Realize the internal equalities such as A'B + A'C = AC.
1 point (content): Proper development of appropriate equations.
1 point (content): Ability to interpret results of work.
1 point (content): Computations on equalities and inequalities are correct.
1 point (clarity): The explanation is clearly written.

13.   ANSWER: There is no triangle since (45 + 30) < 85.

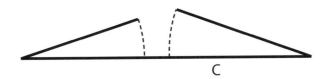

3 possible points
1 point (content): Realize there is no triangle.
1 point (content): Arithmetic is correct.
1 point (clarity): The explanation is clearly written.

CIRCLES AND SPHERES

14.   ANSWER: $\dfrac{2\sqrt{3} - 3}{3}$.

SOLUTION: Join the centers of the circles to get a big equilateral triangle.
Each side of triangle = 2.
Join the center of the central circle to the center of each unit circle.
Little center to tan point distance = r.
Each segment = 1 + r.
Form 6 congruent 30, 60, 90 triangles,
ADG, BDG, BEG, CEG, AFG, CFG.
Each has

      Hypotenuse = 1 + r   ex: $\overline{AG}$

      Leg = $\dfrac{1+r}{2}$ (opp 30 angle = half hypot) ex: $\overline{DG}$

      Leg = 1   ex: $\overline{AD}$

Form 6 more bigger congruent 30, 60, 90 triangles,
ABE, ABF, BCD, BCF, ACD, ACE.
Each has

      Hypotenuse = 2   ex: $\overline{AB}$

      Leg = 1   ex: $\overline{BE}$

      Leg = $\sqrt{3}$ respectively.   ex: $\overline{AE}$

So, $\dfrac{\frac{1+r}{2}}{1} = \dfrac{1}{\sqrt{3}}$

Or $\dfrac{1+r}{2} = \dfrac{1}{\sqrt{3}}$

And $r = \dfrac{2}{\sqrt{3}} - 1 = \dfrac{2\sqrt{3} - 3}{3}$

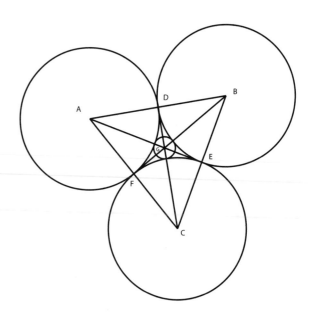

15.   ANSWER: $4 - \sqrt{7}$, or approximately 1.3542 units.

SOLUTION: Since the diameter is 8 units, the radius is 4 units, which is the length of $\overline{AE}$.
Using the Pythagorean theorem, $\overline{AE}^2 = \overline{AB}^2 + \overline{BE}^2$, or $4^2 = \overline{AB}^2 + 3^2$, so $\overline{AB} = \sqrt{7}$. To find $\overline{BC}$,
$\overline{AC} - \overline{AB} = \overline{BC}$. Therefore, $4 - \sqrt{7} = \overline{BC}$.

3 possible points
1 point (content): Realize $\overline{AC} - \overline{AB} = \overline{BC}$.
1 point (content): All arithmetic is correct.
1 point (clarity): The explanation is clearly written.

16.　ANSWER: About 1.6 feet (the answer could vary, depending on what value is used for π).

SOLUTION: Let x be the distance between the equator and the band.

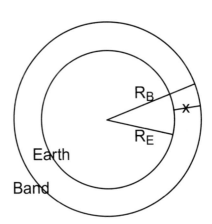

$C = \pi rd = 2\pi r$

$C_{earth} = 25000$ miles

$\qquad = 2\pi r$ miles

$C_{band} = C_{earth} + 10$ feet

$C_{band} = 2\pi(r + x)$

$\qquad = 2\pi r + 2\pi x$

$\cancel{C}_{earth} + 10 \text{ feet} = \cancel{2\pi r} + 2\pi x$

$2\pi r + 10 \text{ feet} = 2\pi r + 2\pi x$

$\qquad 10 \text{ feet} = 2\pi x$

$\qquad x = \dfrac{5}{\pi} \text{ feet} \approx 1.5915 \text{ feet}$

ALTERNATE SOLUTION:

$C_{earth} = 2\pi r_{earth}$ miles

$25000 \text{ miles} = 2\pi r_{earth}$ miles

$(25000)(5280) \text{ feet} = 2\pi r_{earth}$ feet

$\dfrac{132000000}{2\pi} = \dfrac{2\pi r_{earth}}{2\pi}$ in feet

$r_{earth} = 21{,}008{,}452.49$ feet

$(25000)(5280) + 10 \text{ feet} = 2\pi r_{band}$ feet

$\dfrac{132000010}{2\pi} = \dfrac{2\pi r_{band}}{2\pi r}$

$r_{band} = 21008454.08$

$r_{band} - r_{earth} = 21{,}008{,}454.08 \text{ feet} - 21{,}008{,}452.49 \text{ feet}$

$\qquad = 1.589$ feet

4 possible points
1 point (content): Formulas correct.
1 point (content): Setup correct.
1 point (content): Arithmetic correct.
1 point (clarity): The explanation is clearly written.

17.　ANSWER: 12 units.

SOLUTION: The illustration below helps.

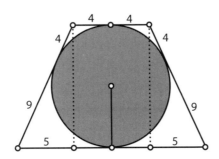

The distance from the short base end to the point of tangency at the top of the circle is 4 units. Similarly, the side point of tangency is 4 units from the short base endpoint. The end of the long base to the point of tangency is half of 18, or 9 units. That means the point of tangency of the isosceles side from the end of the long base is also 9 units. So, the isosceles side is 13 units long. Dropping a perpendicular from the end of the short base to a point on the long base establishes that point as 5 units from the end of the long base. Use the Pythagorean theorem: $d^2 + 5^2 = 13^2$. $d^2 = 169 - 25$, so $d = \sqrt{144}$, or 12 units.

3 possible points
1 point (content): Realize external points are equidistant from points of tangency.
1 point (content): All arithmetic is correct.
1 point (clarity): The explanation is clearly written.

18.   ANSWER: $\sqrt{65}$.

SOLUTION: The center of the circle is the point of intersection of the perpendicular bisectors of the two chords. Since the two chords are perpendicular to each other, you know the chords are parallel to the perpendicular bisectors. With that, you can determine that the point of intersection of the chords is 0.5 units to one side of the center of the circle, measured from the 6, 2 chord and 2 units to the side of the center from the 3, 4 chord. A rectangle is formed between part of the 6, 2 chord and the two perpendicular bisectors with the center of the circle at one corner. The rectangle is 4 by 0.5. Use the Pythagorean theorem to solve for the radius:

$$R^2 = 4^2 + (0.5)^2$$
$$= \frac{65}{4}$$
$$R = \frac{\sqrt{65}}{2}$$
$$D = \sqrt{65}$$

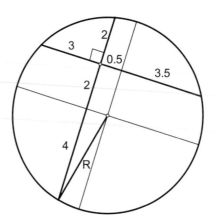

19.   ANSWER: 17 points of intersection.

SOLUTION:

The two circles can intersect at two points. The first line can intersect each circle at two points for a total of 4 points of intersection. The next line can intersect the two circles at 4 points and the first line at one for a total of 5 points of intersection. The last line can intersect the two circles at 4 points, the first line at 1 and the second line at 1 for a total of 6 points of intersection. The grand total of the points of intersection is 2 + 4 + 5 + 6 = 17.

20. SOLUTION: Construct line segments connecting all points to all other points. Since there are only a finite number of points, there will be a finite number of line segments. Each line segment will have an associated slope. However, as there are only a finite number of line segments (slopes), I can pick a different slope from all the others. Construct my line having this slope. Since it is different from all the other slopes, as I pass my line over the circle, my line is guaranteed to only intersect one point at a time. Move the line across the circle until exactly half of the points are on either side of it.

21. ANSWER: $4.00.

    SOLUTION: The area of the first bundle is πr^2, or π since the radius is one. The 2-inch bundle would be worth πr^2, or 4π. Since π is worth a dollar, 4π must be worth $4.00.

    3 possible points
    1 point (content): Realize need to find area of circles.
    1 point (content): Proportion correct.
    1 point (clarity): The explanation is clearly written.

22. ANSWER: The students should provide values close to 3.14 or $\frac{22}{7}$. $\frac{c}{d} = \pi$.

    4 possible points
    1 point (content): Accurate measurements.
    1 point (content): Accurate assumptions.
    1 point (content): Correct generalization.
    1 point (clarity): The explanation is clearly written.

23. ANSWER: 8.5-inch-diameter pizza.

    SOLUTION: It is assumed that the pizza is round. A 6-inch diameter pizza has a radius of 3 inches, giving an area of 9π square inches. Doubling that area so both kids have their fill of pizza means an area of 18π square inches is needed. The area of a circle is πr^2 square inches.
    So, $\pi r^2 = 18\pi$.
    Dividing both sides by π gives $r^2 = 18$.
    So $r = \sqrt{18}$, which is approximately 4.25 inches.
    Thus, the diameter of the pizza needs to be 8.5 inches.

    4 possible points
    1 point (content): Realize need area of 18π.
    1 point (content): Computations are correct.
    1 point (content): Realize the radius needs to be doubled to get the diameter.
    1 point (clarity): The explanation is clearly written.

24.   ANSWER: 703.125 grams.

SOLUTION: The assumption is that the pizza is round. You must consider the pizza areas not just the diameters when you set up a proportion.

$$\frac{450 \text{ grams}}{\text{area of pizza}} = \frac{? \text{ grams}}{\text{area of pizza}}, \text{ where } P = \pi$$

$$\frac{450 \text{ grams}}{\pi 20^2} = \frac{? \text{ grams}}{\pi 25^2}$$

$(450)(\pi)(625) = (?)(\pi)(400)$

$703.125 \text{ grams} = ?$

5 possible points
1 point (content): Realize the need for proportional reasoning.
1 point (content): Substitute the correct values.
1 point (content): The arithmetic is correct.
1 point (clarity): The explanation is clearly written.

25.   ANSWER: About 10.29 units.

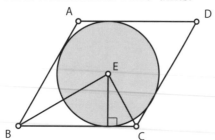

SOLUTION: The diagonals of a rhombus are perpendicular, so $\triangle BEC$ is a right triangle. The diagonals of a rhombus bisect each other.
Since $\overline{BD} = 20$ units, $\overline{BE} = 10$ units.
Since $\overline{AC} = 12$ units, $\overline{CE} = 6$ units.

The area of $\triangle BEC = \dfrac{(10)(6)}{2} = 30$ square units.

$\overline{BC} = \sqrt{10^2 + 6^2} = \sqrt{136} \approx 11.66$

An altitude from point E to $\overline{BC}$ will be the radius of the circle.

The area is 30 square units and also is $\dfrac{(\text{base})(\text{height})}{2}$, or $\dfrac{(11.66)(\text{altitude})}{2} = 30$ square units.

Solving, the altitude = 5.145 units and the diameter = 10.29 units.

5 possible points
1 point (content): Realize rhombus diagonals bisect each other.
1 point (content): Realize rhombus diagonals are perpendicular to each other.
1 point (content): Realize the inscribed circle is tangent to rhombus on each side.
1 point (content): Arithmetic is correct.

1 point (clarity): The explanation is clearly written.

26.   ANSWER: 29.3215 ft, OR 29.3333 ft.

SOLUTION:
C = πd
Circumference of the front wheel (in inches): 14π.
Circumference of the rear wheel (in inches): 16π.
To find the distance traveled before both marks are on the bottom again, determine the least common multiple of both circumferences.
LCM of 14π and 16π is 112π.
Taking LCM, get 352 (using $\frac{22}{7}$ for π) inches or $29.\overline{3}$ ft.

Using 3.1416 for π, you get 29.3216 ft.

3 possible points
1 point (content): Use πd for the circumference.
1 point (content): Calculations and substitutions are correct.
1 point (clarity): The explanation is clearly written.

27.   ANSWER: 6d +πd.

SOLUTION: Extend the straight sides to form a real triangle and see it is equilateral. Two sides are tangent to the corner circles. Construct radii to the tangent points of a corner circle. The quadrilateral formed has two 90 ° angles (tangents) and one 60 ° angle (vertex of equilateral triangle). The central angle formed by the radii must be 120°. So, the string touches $\frac{1}{3}$ of a corner circle's circumference. The three corner circles would mean a total of one circle circumference, or πd, would be touched. Connecting the centers of the circles on one side, the side length at the centers is 2d. But, that is also the distance between the beginning of the curved part at each end, since the two radii in consideration would be perpendicular to the same segment. Thus, the straight sides of the "rounded corner triangle" total 6d. The grand total length of the string is 6d +πd.

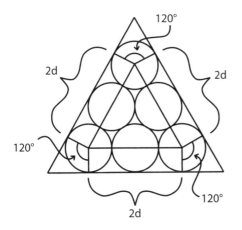

6 possible points

1 point (content): Realize the equilateral triangle.

1 point (content): Realize the angle between radii is 120°.

1 point (content): Realize string touches $\frac{1}{3}$ of a corner circle's circumference.

1 point (content): Realize each straight section of string is 2d long.

1 point (clarity): The explanation is clearly written.

28.   ANSWER: Soccer ball.

SOLUTION:

$$\frac{\text{Mariana Trench}}{\text{Earth Diameter}} = \frac{\text{Seam Depth}}{\text{Ball Diameter}}$$

$$\frac{35{,}640 \text{ feet}}{21{,}008{,}452 \text{ feet}} = \frac{\text{Seam Depth}}{1 \text{ foot}}$$

Converting the fraction to a decimal gives approximately 0.0017 feet, which is about 0.02 inches. Soccer ball seams are deeper than 2 hundredths of an inch.

OR

$$\frac{\text{Mariana Trench + Mt. Everest}}{\text{Earth's Diameter}} = \frac{64{,}940}{21{,}008{,}452}$$

= 0.00309 ft or

= 0.037 in

Including Mount Everest would still make the soccer ball coarser.

4 possible points

1 point (content): Proportions set correctly.

1 point (content): Arithmetic correct.

1 point (content): Conclusion correct.

1 point (clarity): The explanation is clearly written.

29.   ANSWER: 62.5 mph.

SOLUTION: First, to travel 60 miles, find the number of revolutions each tire must make. The 24-inch tires have a circumference ($C = \pi d$) of 75.398 inches. There are $\left(\frac{60 \text{ miles}}{1}\right)\left(\frac{5280 \text{ feet}}{\text{mile}}\right) = \left(\frac{12 \text{ inches}}{\text{foot}}\right)$ 3,801,600 inches in 60 miles. For the 24-inch tire to travel 60 miles, each tire revolves $\frac{3801600}{75.398} = 50{,}420.4$ times. The new tires have a circumference of 78.54 inches. For the 25-inch tire to travel 60 miles, each tire revolves $\frac{3801600}{78.54} = 48{,}403.36$ times. $\frac{50420.4}{48403.36}$ shows that the smaller tire revolves 1.04167 times greater. (1.04167)(60) = 62.5 mph with the 25-inch tires on when the car reads 60 mph.

OR

The 25-inch tires would travel (50,420.4)(78.54) = 3,960,018.22 inches. 3,960,018.22 divided by 12 gives 330,001.5 feet. 330,001.5 divided by 5280 gives 62.5 miles. This is the distance the car would travel in one hour. Your actual speed would be 62.5 mph.

OR

$$\frac{? \text{ mph}}{60 \text{ mph}} = \frac{25"}{24"}$$

$$\frac{x}{60} = \frac{25}{24}$$

$$\frac{x}{60} = 1.041\overline{6}$$

$$x = 60(1.04\overline{6})$$

$$x = 62.5 \text{ mph}$$

30. SOLUTION: Draw two diameters. This will divide the original circle into 4 parts. Then, draw one concentric circle, which along with the two diameters divides the original circle into eight parts. Notice that nothing stipulates the parts have to be equal in size. The difficult part for this solution is the realization that there needs to be a second circle.

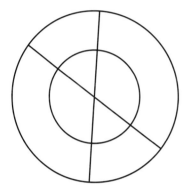

3 possible points
1 point (content): Realize need for two diameters.
1 point (content): Realize the need for second concentric circle.
1 point (clarity): The explanation is clearly written.

31. SOLUTION: Draw two diameters perpendicular to each other. Then, draw one concentric circle. If the radius of the large circle is one unit, then its area must be $\pi r^2 = \pi(1)^2 = \pi$. If the area of the small circle is to be $\dfrac{\pi}{2}$, then:

$$A = \pi r^2$$

$$\frac{\pi}{2} = \pi r^2$$

$$\left(\frac{\pi}{2}\right)\left(\frac{1}{\pi}\right) = \left(\frac{\pi r^2}{2}\right)\left(\frac{1}{\pi}\right)$$

$$\frac{1}{2} = r^2$$

$$\sqrt{\frac{1}{2}} = r$$

$$\left(\sqrt{\frac{1}{2}}\right)\left(\sqrt{\frac{2}{2}}\right) = r$$

$$\frac{\sqrt{2}}{2} = r$$

Now, the area of the smaller circle is $\pi r^2 = \pi\left(\dfrac{\sqrt{2}}{2}\right)^2 = \pi\left(\dfrac{2}{4}\right) = \dfrac{\pi}{2}$. But that makes the area surrounding the ring $\dfrac{\pi}{2}$ also. Quartering either of those gives an area of $\left(\dfrac{\pi}{8}\right)$. Between the sections in the small circle and the sections in the "donut", the total area is $8\left(\dfrac{\pi}{8}\right)$, which is π.

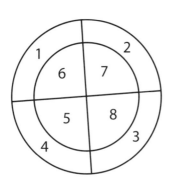

The sum of the areas of each of the sections 1, 2, 3, 4, 5, 6, 7, and 8 would be $\frac{\pi}{8} + \frac{\pi}{8} + \frac{\pi}{8} + \frac{\pi}{8} + \frac{\pi}{8} + \frac{\pi}{8} + \frac{\pi}{8} + \frac{\pi}{8}$, or π.

4 possible points
1 point (content): Realize need for two diameters.
1 point (content): Realize the need for second concentric circle.
1 point (content): Realize need for diameters to be perpendicular.
1 point (clarity): The explanation is clearly written.

32.   ANSWER: R = $10\sqrt{5} - 20$ or 2.3606798 or 2.36 or even 2.4 or $\frac{10}{2 + \sqrt{5}}$

SOLUTION:

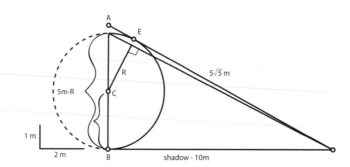

Visualize a vertical cut of the sphere perpendicular to the surface, passing through the center so you have a great circle. Run a vertical segment ($\overline{AB}$) from the point of contact (B) between the circle and the surface, through the center of the circle (C). Point A will be above the top of the circle. Since the meter stick casts a 2 m long shadow and the sphere casts a 10 m shadow, it must be the case that $\overline{AB}$ is 5 m long (from the 1:2 ratio of the meter stick and its shadow). You now have a big right triangle with a base of 10 and a height of 5, making the hypotenuse, $\overline{AD}$ be $5\sqrt{5}$ (from the Pythagorean theorem). The hypotenuse of the big triangle is tangent to the circle at point E ($\overline{CE}$ is the radius, R). Since $\triangle$CEA is similar to $\triangle$DBA, the ratios of the corresponding sides will be equal.

Thus, $\dfrac{\overline{CE}}{\overline{AC}} = \dfrac{\overline{BD}}{\overline{AD}}$

or $\dfrac{R}{5 - R} = \dfrac{10}{5\sqrt{5}} = \dfrac{2}{\sqrt{5}}$

In other words, $\dfrac{R}{5 - R} = \dfrac{2}{\sqrt{5}}$

and $R\sqrt{5} = 2(5 - R)$
or $R\sqrt{5} = 10 - 2R$

and $R(\sqrt{5} + 2) = 10$

Thus, $R = \left(\dfrac{10}{\sqrt{5} + 2}\right)\left(\dfrac{\sqrt{5} + 2}{\sqrt{5} + 2}\right)$

$= \dfrac{10(\sqrt{5} - 2)}{(\sqrt{5})^2 - 2^2}$

and $R = 10\sqrt{5} - 20$.

This answer could be expressed as 2.3606798 or 2.36 or even 2.4.

33.   ANSWER: 2π

SOLUTION: The two ends make a circle. Lane 1 would have a circumference of C_1 and Lane 2 would have a circumference of C_2. So, the difference between the two lanes is independent of the lengths of the straight sections, so $D = C_2 - C_1$. If R is the radius of the circle with circumference C_1 in meters, then $R + 1$ is the radius of the circle with circumference C_2.

$C_1 = 2\pi R$ $c = \pi d$
$C_2 = 2\pi(R+1)$
$D = C_2 - C_1$
$\quad = 2\pi(R+1) - 2\pi R$
$\quad = 2\pi R + 2\pi - 2\pi R$
$\quad = 2\pi$

Rubric
4 possible points
1 point (content): Realize that the two ends make a circle.
1 point (content): Realize that the straights do not impact the conclusions.
1 point (content): Formulas and computations used correctly.
1 point (clarity): The explanation is clearly written.

CONSTRUCTIONS

34.   ANSWER: Altitudes are concurrent (meet at a common point) inside or outside the triangle.

SOLUTION: Some possible sketches are:

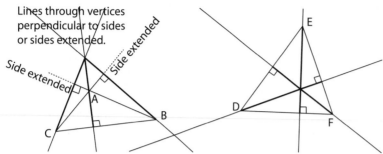

Note that the thick segments are the altitudes.   The altitudes meet outside triangle ABC and inside triangle DEF.

3 possible points
1 point (content): Altitudes are drawn correctly.
1 point (content): Both possibilities are shown.
1 point (clarity): The explanation is clearly written or the sketch is clearly drawn.

35.   ANSWER: Angle bisectors are concurrent (meet at a common point) inside the triangle.

SOLUTION: Some possible sketches are:

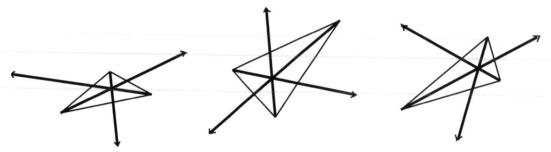

Note that the thick rays are the angle bisectors.

3 possible points
1 point (content): State that the angle bisectors are concurrent.
1 point (content): State that the common point is always inside the triangle.
1 point (clarity): The explanation is clearly written or the sketch is clearly drawn.

36.   ANSWER: Medians are concurrent (meet at a common point) inside the triangle.

SOLUTION: Some possible sketches are:

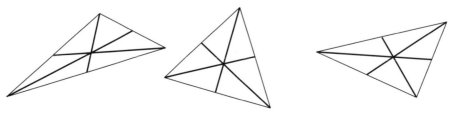

Note that the thick segments are the medians.

3 possible points
1 point (content): Medians are drawn correctly.
1 point (content): State that the medians meet at a common point.
1 point (clarity): The explanation is clearly written or the sketch is clearly drawn.

37. ANSWER: Medians are concurrent (meet at a common point) inside the triangle. The ratio of the lengths of the segments on either side of the point of concurrence on one of the medians is 2:1 or 1:2. Notice in the example below that the $\overline{AB}$ = 3.75 in. and $\overline{BC}$ = 1.88 in., which when doubled is 3.76 in. This apparent discrepancy is a result of rounding that is done within the software used to create the figure. However, similar rounding occurs during any measurement and it is important to note that fact.

SOLUTION: A possible sketch is:

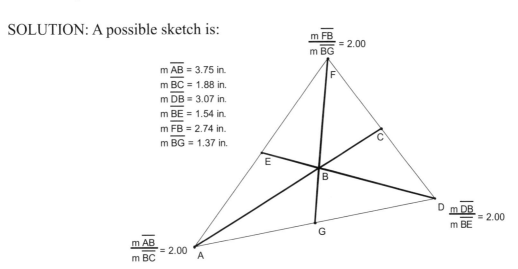

Note that the thick segments are the medians.

3 possible points
1 point (content): Medians are drawn correctly.
1 point (content): State that the medians meet at a common point.
1 point (clarity): The explanation is clearly written or the sketch is clearly drawn.

38. ANSWER: Midlines are concurrent (meet at a common point) inside or outside the triangle.

SOLUTION: Some possible sketches are:

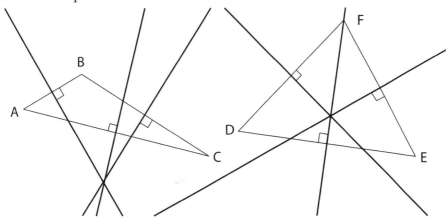

Note that the thick segments are the midlines. The midlines meet outside triangle ABC and inside triangle DEF.

3 possible points
1 point (content): Midlines are drawn correctly.
1 point (content): Both possibilities are shown.
1 point (clarity): The explanation is clearly written or the sketch is clearly drawn.

39.   ANSWER: Yes.

SOLUTION: Some possible sketches are:

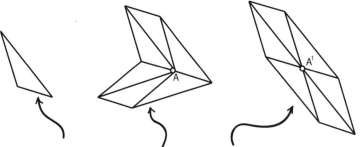

Using this triangle will give this shape OR this shape, among others.

3 possible points
1 point (content): Realize that the sum of the angles at points A and A^1 equals 360°.
1 point (content): Yes, it can be done.
1 point (clarity): The explanation is clearly written or the sketch is clearly drawn.

40.   SOLUTION: The toothpicks will form a tetrahedron (3-dimensional figure made up of four equilateral triangles). This is a sufficient response if no sketch is provided.

If a sketch is shown, it will be made with six segments, and although the sketch will show two different lengths (due to the limitation of showing a 3-dimensional object in 2-dimensional space), they will all be assumed to be the same length.

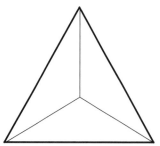

The thin segments in the sketch are either protruding out from the page, or are sinking into the background of the page. All six segments would be the same length in 3-space.

2 possible points
1 point (content): Realize the need for 3-dimensional solution.
1 point (clarity): The explanation is clearly written or the sketch is clearly drawn.

41. Many solutions are possible.

Example of an answer:

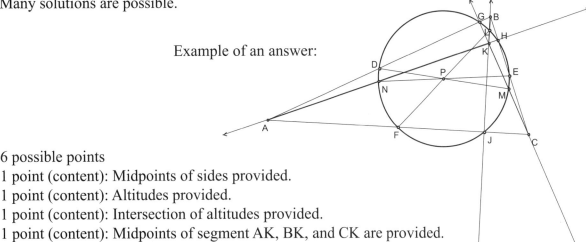

6 possible points
1 point (content): Midpoints of sides provided.
1 point (content): Altitudes provided.
1 point (content): Intersection of altitudes provided.
1 point (content): Midpoints of segment AK, BK, and CK are provided.
1 point (content): Center of circle provided.
1 point (clarity): The explanation is clearly written or the sketch is clearly drawn.

42. SOLUTION:

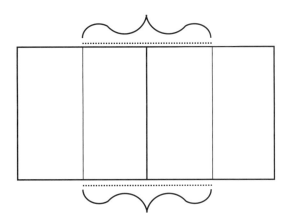

Two squares are shown with the thick segments and use 7 toothpicks. A third square is shown with the two thin parallel segments (using two more toothpicks) and the portion of the thick segments parallel to the dashed segments). Thus, a total of nine toothpicks are used to create three congruent squares.

3 possible points
1 point (content): Realize the need for the overlapping third square.
1 point (content): Realize two sides of one square are formed by using two half-toothpicks.
1 point (clarity): The explanation is clearly written or the sketch is clearly drawn.

43. SOLUTION:

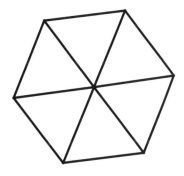

3 possible points
1 point (content): Realize the need to make equilateral triangles.
1 point (content): Realize the result is a regular hexagon.
1 point (clarity): The sketch represents the solution.

44. ANSWER: 6, 5, and 4 toothpick-lengths on a side each give one square. Three toothpick-lengths on a side gives three squares (two with 3 toothpick side lengths and one with 1 toothpick side length). Two toothpick-lengths on a side give seven squares (three with 2 toothpick side lengths and four with 1 toothpick side lengths). One toothpick length per side gives 6 or 7 squares, depending upon the configuration used.

SOLUTION:

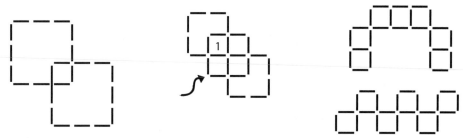

7 possible points
1 point (content): One 6 toothpick side length square.
1 point (content): One 5 toothpick side length square.
1 point (content): One 4 toothpick side length square.
1 point (content): Three 3 toothpick side length squares.
1 point (content): Seven 2 toothpick side length squares.
1 point (content): Six or seven 1 toothpick side length squares.
1 point (clarity): The explanation is clearly written or the sketch is clearly drawn.
Bonus point: Both answers are given for 1 toothpick side length squares.

45. ANSWER: The exterior sides form a straight angle.

SOLUTION: A+B+C = 180º

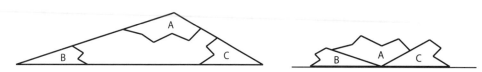

3 possible points
1 point (content): Vertices are torn off correctly.
1 point (content): Vertices arranged to show straight angle.
1 point (clarity): The explanation is clearly written or the sketch is clearly drawn.

46. SOLUTION: Cut in a stair step fashion. Starting at the top left corner, go along the top edge of the 16-foot length for 4 feet. From that point, make a cut parallel to the 9-foot edge that is 3 feet long. Turn left 90º and make a cut parallel to the 16-foot edge that is 4 feet long. Turn right 90º make a cut parallel to the 9-foot edge that is 3 feet long. Turn left 90º and make a cut parallel to the 16-foot edge that is 4 feet long. Turn right 90º and make a cut parallel to the 9-foot edge that is 3 feet long. At this point, you will exit the carpet 4 feet from the bottom right corner of the carpet.

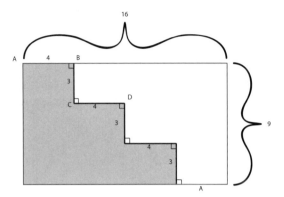

To make a 12 feet by 12 feet square, move the shaded segment of carpet so that $\overline{AB}$ is located where $\overline{CD}$ is in the above figure.

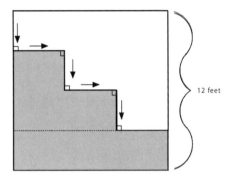

47.   ANSWER: The measure of the inscribed angle (MHN because all three points are on the circle) is half that of the central angle (vertex is the center of the circle). Or, it could be said that the measure of the central angle is twice that of the measure of the inscribed angle.

SOLUTION: Some possible sketches are:

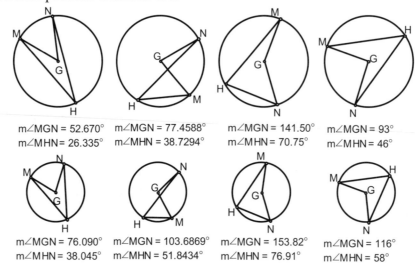

m∠MGN = 52.670° m∠MGN = 77.4588° m∠MGN = 141.50° m∠MGN = 93°
m∠MHN = 26.335° m∠MHN = 38.7294° m∠MHN = 70.75°   m∠MHN = 46°

m∠MGN = 76.090° m∠MGN = 103.6869° m∠MGN = 153.82° m∠MGN = 116°
m∠MHN = 38.045° m∠MHN = 51.8434°   m∠MHN = 76.91°   m∠MHN = 58°

Notice that sometimes the ratio is not exactly 2:1 (or 1:2) because of rounding (look at the top right circle). This rounding occurs with any measurement but can appear more dramatic with dynamic software because the rounding sometimes goes unnoticed. For all cases shown here, $\dfrac{m\angle MGN}{m\angle MHN} = \dfrac{2}{1}$, regardless of the precision, and it is because of the rounding.

4 possible points
1 point (content): Constructions are correct.
1 point (content): Angles are measured correctly.
1 point (content): Correct ratio conjecture (2:1 or 1:2) is established.
1 point (clarity): The explanation is clearly written or the sketch is clearly drawn.

48.   SOLUTION:

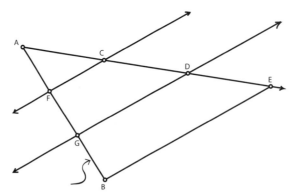

Draw segment $\overline{AB}$. Create $\overrightarrow{AC}$. Mark off $\overline{CD}$ on $\overrightarrow{AC}$ so that $\overline{CD}$ is the same length as $\overline{AC}$. Mark off $\overline{DE}$ on $\overrightarrow{AC}$ so that $\overline{DE}$ is the same length as $\overline{AC}$. Make $\overline{BE}$. Construct a line parallel to $\overline{BE}$ through point C, calling the intersection with $\overline{AB}$ point F. Construct a line parallel to $\overline{BE}$ through point D, calling the intersection with segment $\overline{AB}$ point G. $\overleftrightarrow{FC}$ and $\overleftrightarrow{GD}$ are parallel to $\overline{BE}$. There is a theorem in geometry that states that lines parallel to a side of a triangle divide the other two sides of the triangle in equally proportional sections. Since $\overline{AE}$ is divided into thirds, $\overline{AB}$ must also be divided into thirds.

4 possible points
1 point (content): Realize the need to create a new segment divided into thirds.
1 point (content): Realize the need to make segment BE.
1 point (content): Realize the need for lines parallel to segment BE.
1 point (clarity): The explanation is clearly written.

49. ANSWER: The number of sets that will form a triangle will vary. The probability will vary depending on the number of sets that result in a triangle. As this is done with a group, the results and probabilities will change. The sum of the measures of two lengths of the sides must be greater than the third side to make a triangle (this leads to the triangle inequality).

As this activity is done, the person can be asked to use only one piece of stick spaghetti initially. Typically, the first time the individual attempts to create three congruent pieces. After that, ask the individual to not make the pieces be the same length.

SOLUTION: Some possible sketches are:

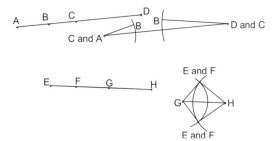

4 possible points
1 point (content): Realize ABCD will not yield a triangle because $(\overline{AB} + \overline{BC}) < \overline{CD}$.
1 point (content): Realize EFGH gives a triangle because $(\overline{EF} + \overline{FG}) > \overline{GH}$.
1 point (content): Generalize correctly.
1 point (clarity): The explanation is clearly written or the sketch is clearly drawn.

50. 5 possible points
1 point (content): Circle projects an ellipse.
1 point (content): Square projects an isosceles trapezoid (assuming centered).
1 point (content): Rectangle projects an isosceles trapezoid (assuming centered).
1 point (content): Equilateral triangle projects isosceles triangle (assuming centered).
1 point (clarity): The explanation is clearly written.
Bonus point: Flashlight could be used instead of strings to show projection.

51. SOLUTION:

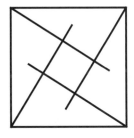

3 possible points
1 point (content): Realize that four toothpicks are inside the large square.
1 point (content): Realize that internal toothpick pairs must be parallel.
1 point (clarity): The explanation is clearly written.

52.   ANSWER: A regular hexagon.

SOLUTION: Six of the segments around the outside and 6 as spokes out from the center to each of six respective vertices. Here the congruent regions would be equilateral triangles.

If three of the "spoke" segments of the regular hexagon are hidden, the figure becomes a cube, which would also satisfy the conditions of the problem. Here the congruent regions would be squares.

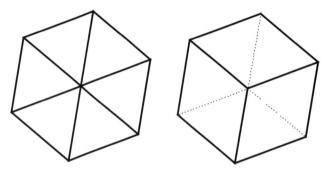

3 possible points
1 point (content): Realize that the figure is a regular hexagon.
1 point (content): Realize that the "spokes" and edges form equilateral triangles.
1 point (clarity): The explanation is clearly written.
BONUS point: Second solution – it could be the case that someone will do the cube first and then the regular hexagon.

53.   ANSWER: AAA and SSA do not always give congruent triangles.

SOLUTION:

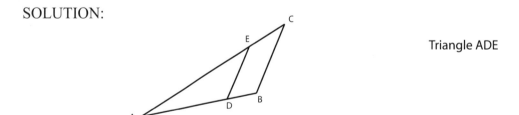

Triangle ADE

Triangles ADE and ABC share AAA, but they are not congruent.

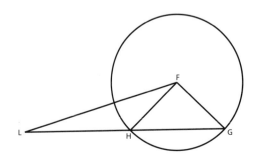

∠FLH and side $\overline{FL}$ are constant. Sides $\overline{FH}$ and $\overline{FG}$ are congruent because they are radii of the circle. ΔFLH and ΔFLG share SSA, but they are not congruent.

4 possible points
1 point (content): Constructions for AAA are correct.
1 point (content): Constructions for SSA are correct.
1 point (content): Both answers are given.
1 point (clarity): The explanation is clearly written

ANGLES

54.   ANSWER: 360°.

SOLUTION: Put a parallel line (RS) through the point P of the transversals.

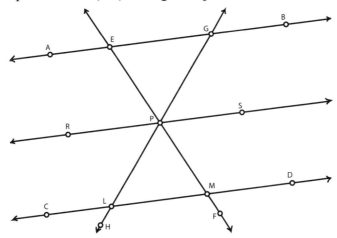

m∠BGP + m∠EGB = 180°   supplementary angles
m∠EGP = m∠GPS   alternate interior angles of parallel lines
m∠BGP + m∠GPS = 180°   substitute ∠GPS for ∠EGB
m∠DMP + m∠LMP = 180°   supplementary angles
m∠LMP = m∠MPS   alternate interior angles of parallel lines
m∠DMP + m∠MPS = 180°   substitute ∠GPS for ∠EGB
m∠MPS + m∠BGP = m∠GPM   adjacent angles
m∠BGP + m∠GPM + m∠DMP = 180° + 180°   substitution
m∠BGP + m∠GPM + m∠DMP = 360°   arithmetic

55.   ANSWER: 100°.

SOLUTION: We know∠DBC + ∠DCB + ∠BDC = ∠DBC + ∠DCB + ∠140°.
But ∠DBC + ∠DCB + ∠BDC = 180°.
So ∠DBC + ∠DCB + 140° = 180°.
And ∠DBC + ∠DCB = 40°.
But that sum of 40° is half of ∠ABC + ∠ACB, making ∠ABC + ∠ACB = 80° and the remaining angle in triangle ABC, ∠BAC = 100°.

5 possible points
1 point (content): Realize the need to start with triangle BCD.
1 point (content): Realize that $\angle DBC + \angle DCB = 40°$.
1 point (content): Realize that $\angle ABC + \angle ACB = 80°$.
1 point (content): Realize that $\angle BAC = 100°$.
1 point (clarity): The explanation is clearly written.

56.　　ANSWER: Approximately 15.35 cm2.

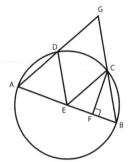

SOLUTION: $\overline{EC}$ and $\overline{EB}$ are radii of the circle, making $\triangle BCE$ isosceles. But, m$\angle EBC$ is 60° because $\triangle ABC$ is isosceles. That means m$\angle EBC$ is 60°, since $\triangle BCE$ isosceles with base angles EBC and ECB. $\overline{CF}$ is an altitude of $\triangle BCE$, making $\triangle BCF$ a 30-60-90 right triangle (altitude of an isosceles triangle bisects the vertex angle, so m$\angle BCF$ is $\dfrac{60°}{2}$ = 30°, m$\angle BFC$ = 90° ($\overline{CF} \perp \overline{EB}$), and m$\angle EBC$ is 60° because $\triangle ABC$ is isosceles). The altitude of an isosceles triangle bisects the base too, so segment $\overline{FB}$ is 2.5 cm long. Side $\overline{CB}$ is 5 cm long because $\triangle BCE$ is isosceles. The Pythagorean theorem is used to find the length of $\overline{CF}$ (m$(\overline{CF})^2$ + m$(\overline{FB})^2$ = m$(\overline{BC})^2$ or m$(\overline{CF})^2$ + $2.5^2 = 5^2$ and m$(\overline{CF})^2$ = 25 - 6.25 = 18.75 cm. Thus, m$\overline{CF} = \sqrt{18.75}$, which is approximately 4.33 cm. The area of $\triangle BCE$ is $\dfrac{bh}{2} = \dfrac{(2.5 \text{ cm})(4.83 \text{ cm})}{2} \approx 5.41$ cm^2.

Using similar reasoning, $\triangle ADE$ must be equilateral with an area of ≈ 5.41 cm^2.

Since $\triangle BCE$ and $\triangle ADE$ are equilateral, $\angle DEC$ must be 60° because $\overline{AB}$ is a diameter and thus a straight line segment. In this case, the area of a circle is πr^2 or (3.14)(25 cm). Thus, the area of the circle is ≈ 78.5 cm^2. The area of sector DEC is $\dfrac{1}{6}$ of the area of the circle, or $\dfrac{78.5 \text{ cm}^2}{6}$, since the interior angle is 60°. Thus, the area of the sector is ≈ 13.08 cm^2. The area of the region in question is the area of $\triangle ADE$ + the area of $\triangle BCE$ + the area of sector DEC, or approximately 5.41 cm^2 + 5.41 cm^2 + 13.08 cm^2, which is 23.9 cm^2.

The area of the semi-circle is approximately $\dfrac{78.5 \text{ cm}^2}{2}$, or 39.25 cm^2. Subtracting 23.9 cm^2 from 39.25 cm^2 gives approximately 15.35 cm^2 for the area of the two shaded regions.

8 possible points
1 point (content): Realize ∆BCE is equilateral.
1 point (content): Compute the length of altitude $\overline{CF}$ correctly.
1 point (content): Compute the area of ∆BCE correctly.
1 point (content): Realize ∆BCE and ∆ADE are congruent.
1 point (content): Realize the area of the sector CED is of the circle.
1 point (content): Compute the area of sector CED correctly.
1 point (content): Realize need to subtract the areas from the semi-circle area.
1 point (clarity): The explanation is clearly written or the sketch is clearly drawn.

57.   Answer: 15°.

SOLUTION: Redrawing the construction shows:

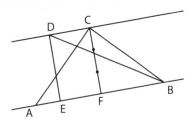

Since $\overline{AC}$ is congruent to $\overline{BC}$ and ∠ACB = 90°, then ∠CAB and ∠ABC = 45°. $\overline{DE}$ and $\overline{CF}$ are perpendicular to $\overline{AB}$. $\overline{CD}$ bisects $\overline{AB}$. Therefore, $\overline{DE} = \overline{CF} = \overline{AF} = \left(\frac{1}{2}\right)(\overline{AB}) = \left(\frac{1}{2}\right)(\overline{BD})$. Therefore ∆BDE is a 30-60-90 triangle. Then ∠DBE = 30°. ∠DBE + ∠CBD = ∠ABC, then 30 + ∠CBD = 45. ∠CBD = 15.

58.   SOLUTION: $\overline{AD} + \overline{AB} = \overline{AD} + \overline{AD} + \overline{DE} + \overline{BE}$
$$= 2\overline{AD} + 2\overline{DE}$$
$$= 2AE$$
$$\overline{AE} = \frac{\overline{AD} + \overline{AB}}{2}$$

∆ADC is similar to ∆ABC (both are right triangles, both contain ∠A)

so $\dfrac{\overline{AD}}{\overline{AC}} = \dfrac{\overline{AC}}{\overline{AB}}$

and $AC = \sqrt{(\overline{AD})(\overline{AB})} < \dfrac{\overline{AD} + \overline{AB}}{2}$

But $\dfrac{\overline{AD} + \overline{AB}}{2} = AE$, so $\overline{AC} < \overline{AE}$.

$\overline{AC} < \overline{AE}$ implies the measure of ∠ACS > the measure of ∠AEC because the larger angle of a triangle will be opposite the longer side.

3 possible points
1 point (content): Use similar triangles in proof.
1 point (content): Calculations and substitutions are correct.
1 point (clarity): The explanation is clearly written.

59.   ANSWER: 58°.

SOLUTION: The two extremes exist where the angles measures would be $1° + 2° + 177°$ and $59° + 60° + 61°$. The first produces a sum of 179° for the two largest angles and the second produces a sum of 121°. The difference is 179° - 121° = 58°.

4 possible points
1 point (content): Realize one extreme is $1° + 2° + 177°$.
1 point (content): Realize one extreme is $59° + 60° + 61°$.
1 point (content): Realize the need to add the two largest angles in each extreme.
1 point (clarity): The explanation is clearly written.

60.   Draw $\overline{CD}$ perpendicular to $\overline{AB}$. $\triangle ACD$ is a right triangle with $\angle A = 30°$. Since $\sin 30° = 0.5$, $\overline{CD} = 0.5\ \overline{AC}$. But since M is the midpoint of $\overline{AC}$, $\overline{MC} = \overline{MA} = \overline{CD}$. That makes the measure of $\angle ACD$ 60° and $\triangle CMD$ is equilateral so $\overline{DM} = \overline{MC} = \overline{MA} = \overline{CD}$. The measure of $\angle DCB$ is 45°. Since $\triangle AMD$ is isosceles and the measure of $\angle A$ is 30°, the measure of $\angle ADM$ must also be 30°. That makes the measure of $\angle BDM = 150°$. But, $\triangle BDM$ is isosceles because $\overline{BD} = \overline{DM}$, so the measure of both $\angle MBD$ and $\angle BMD$ is 15°. Since the measure of $\angle DBC = 45°$, subtracting 15 for the measure of $\angle DBM$ leaves 30° for the measure of $\angle MBC$. And $\overline{AB} = \overline{AE}$. In $\triangle ADB$, $\overline{BD} = 0.5\ \overline{AB}$, $\overline{MD} = 0.5\ \overline{AE} = 0.5\ \overline{AB}$. $\angle MBD$ is 45°. Remove $\angle DBC$ and get $\angle MBC$ is 30°.

5 possible points
1 point (content): Realize the need to construct $\overline{CD}$.
1 point (content): Realize that $\triangle CDM$ is equilateral.
1 point (content): Realize that $\triangle ADM$ is isosceles.
1 point (content): Realize that $\triangle BDM$ is isosceles.
1 point (clarity): The explanation is clearly written.

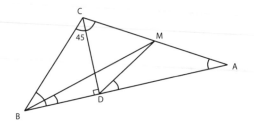

61.   ANSWER: 75°.

SOLUTION: Let E be a point on $\overline{AD}$ such that $\overline{CE}$ is perpendicular to $\overline{AD}$, and draw $\overline{BE}$. Since $\angle ADC$ is an exterior angle of $\triangle ADB$, $\angle ADC = (\angle DAB + \angle ABD) = (15° + 45°) = 60°$. Thus, $\triangle CDE$ is a 30-60-90 triangle and $\overline{DE} = 0.5\overline{CD} = \overline{BD}$.
Hence, $\triangle BDE$ is isosceles and $\angle EBD = \angle BED = 30°$.
But $\angle ECB$ is also equal to 30°.
Therefore $\triangle BEC$ is isosceles, with $\overline{BE} = \overline{CE}$.
However, $\angle ABE = \angle ABD - \angle EBD = 45° - 30° = 15° = \angle EAB$.
Thus, $\triangle ABE$ is isosceles, with $\overline{AE} = \overline{BE}$. Hence, $\overline{AE} = \overline{BE} = \overline{CE}$.

The ΔAEC is right and also isosceles, with ∠EAC = ∠ECA = 45°.
∠ACB = ∠ECA + ∠ECD = 45° + 30° = 75°.
Hence,

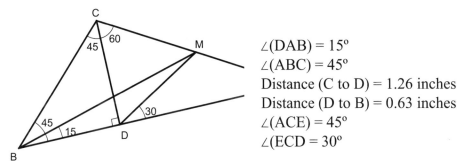

∠(DAB) = 15°
∠(ABC) = 45°
Distance (C to D) = 1.26 inches
Distance (D to B) = 0.63 inches
∠(ACE) = 45°
∠(ECD = 30°

AREA AND PERIMETER

62.   ANSWER: $\sqrt{8}$ or about 2.828.

SOLUTION: There is only one triangle that would satisfy this condition. If the perimeter is 8, then $a + b + c = 8$. We know the sum of the lengths of two sides must be greater than the length of the third side. If one side is 4, the sum of the other two side lengths would be 4, which cannot be. Therefore the side lengths must 1, 2, or 3. At least two side lengths must be 3 or the perimeter would be less than 8. Therefore, the only possible triangle is isosceles with side lengths 3, 3, and 2. If 2 is the base, then the altitude bisects the base and from the Pythagorean theorem, the height is $\sqrt{8}$. The area is $\dfrac{(\text{base})(\text{height})}{2} = \dfrac{(2)(\sqrt{8})}{2}$ or $\sqrt{8}$.

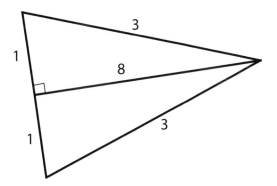

6 possible points
1 point (content): Recognize side lengths must be less than 4.
1 point (content): Recognize the only triangle is isosceles (side lengths 3, 3, & 2).
1 point (content): Remember the altitude bisects the base in a right angle.
1 point (content): Altitude correctly computed.
1 point (content): Area correctly computed.
1 point (clarity): Explanation is clearly written or sketch is clearly drawn.

63.   ANSWER: 4.5293 CM².

— SOLUTION: Draw circle O with diameter A and B. Make the third vertex of the triangle C, and the intersection of the triangle and the circle between B and C be D. Make the intersection of the triangle and the circle between A and C be E. ΔODB and ΔOEA are both isosceles ($\overline{OB}$, $\overline{OD}$, $\overline{OA}$, and $\overline{OE}$ are each radii). But $\angle$OBD and $\angle$OAE both measure 60°, so ΔODB and ΔOEA must be equilateral as well. Their common side length is 5 cm, the radius of the circle. Thus, each triangle has an area of $\dfrac{25\sqrt{3}}{4}$. The area of sector OBD is $\dfrac{1}{6}$ the area of the circle, or $\dfrac{25\pi}{6}$.

Thus, the area of the region in question is $2\left(\dfrac{25\pi}{6} - \dfrac{25\sqrt{3}}{4}\right) = 4.5293$ cm².

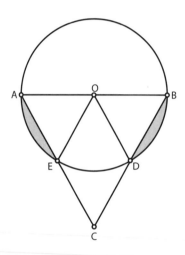

64.   ANSWER: $A = \pi r^2$, $AB = \pi r$.

SOLUTION: The formula for the area of a parallelogram is length times width, or base times height. Here, the length or base length is πr and the width or height is r. So, $A = (l)(w) = (\pi r)(r) = \pi r^2$. Or, $A = (b)(h) = (\pi r)(r) = \pi r^2$.

5 possible points
1 point (content): Realize long side length = πr (half the circumference of $2\pi r$).
1 point (content): Realize the height of the parallelogram is r.
1 point (content): Use formula for area of parallelogram.
1 point (content): Conclude area is πr^2.
1 point (clarity): The explanation is clearly written.

65.   ANSWER: 82.7% and 82.7% (accept 82.6 to 82.8).

SOLUTION: The shaded area in the figure is NOT part of the overlapping regions.

 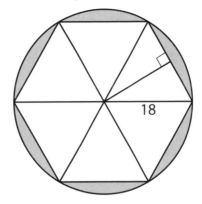

The regular hexagon is made up of 6 equilateral triangles.
In the smaller circle, the side lengths of the triangles are 6 inches/any random measure.
The altitude of one of the triangles is $3^2 + x^2 = 6^2$ (Pythagorean theorem)
$9 + x^2 = 69$, $x^2 = 36 - 9$, $x = \sqrt{27} \approx 5.196$

$\sqrt{62-35} = \sqrt{27} \approx 5.196$, OR $3\sqrt{3}$.

Easier Solution:
Let 4 = 1, a unit circle.

The area of one triangle is $\dfrac{(5.196)(6)}{2} \approx 15.588$.

The regular hexagon has area $(6)(15.588) \approx 93.531$.
The area of the circle is $(36)(3.14) \approx 113.04$.
$\dfrac{93.531}{113.04} \approx 82.7\%$

The ratio is independent of the size of the circle since all computations are in terms of the radius.
You would still get a percentage of 82.7 if the radius changed.

5 possible points
1 point (content): Altitude is computed correctly.
1 point (content): Area of hexagon and circle are computed correctly .
1 point (content): Ratio is computed correctly.
1 point (content): Realize the ratio is independent of the radius length.
1 point (clarity): The explanation is clearly written.
*Bonus Point: Confirm by an algebra ratio that is independent of the size of the circle.

66.   ANSWER: Approximately 2.92 square units.

SOLUTION:

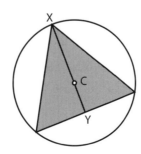

101

Let C be the center of the circle, Y the midpoint of a side of the triangle, and X the vertex of the triangle opposite the side having Y as a midpoint. A circumference of 3π also equals $2\pi r$, so $3\pi = 2\pi r$. Solving for the radius of the circle, $r = \dfrac{3\pi}{2\pi} = \dfrac{3}{2}$. Then $\overline{XC}$, which is a radius, $= \dfrac{3}{2}$. Also, since the center of the circle is the circumcenter of the inscribed equilateral triangle, we know that $\overline{XC}$ is $\dfrac{2}{3}$ of $\overline{XY}$ (or, the center of the circumscribed circle would be located $\dfrac{2}{3}$ of the way from the vertex on the median $\overline{XY}$). So, $\overline{XC} = \overline{XY}$. But, $\overline{XC} = \dfrac{3}{2}$, so $\dfrac{3}{2} = \dfrac{2}{3}\,\overline{XY}$. Solving for $\overline{XY}$, the length is $\dfrac{9}{4}$. If a is the length of each side of the triangle, then the Pythagorean theorem gives $(\overline{XY})^2 + \left(\dfrac{a}{2}\right)^2 = a^2$ and the area of the triangle is $\left(\dfrac{1}{2}\right)\left(\dfrac{9}{4}\right)a$. Solving for a in the Pythagorean equation gives:

$$\left(\dfrac{9}{4}\right)^2 + \left(\dfrac{a}{2}\right)^2 = a^2$$

$$\dfrac{81}{16} + \dfrac{a^2}{4} = a^2$$

$$\dfrac{81}{16} + \dfrac{4a^2}{16} = \dfrac{16a^2}{16}$$

$$\dfrac{81}{16} = \dfrac{16a^2 - 4a^2}{16}$$

$$81 = 12a^2$$

$$\sqrt{\dfrac{81}{12}} = a$$

$$\dfrac{3\sqrt{3}}{2} = a$$

Then the area of the triangle is $\left(\dfrac{1}{2}\right)\left(\dfrac{9}{4}\right)\left(\dfrac{3\sqrt{3}}{2}\right)\left(\dfrac{27\sqrt{3}}{16}\right) \approx 2.92$ square units.

5 possible points

1 point (content): Realize $3\pi = 2\pi r$.

1 point (content): Realize $XC = \dfrac{2}{3}XY$.

1 point (content): Realize need to solve $(XY)^2 + \left(\dfrac{2}{3}\right)^2 = a^2$.

1 point (content): Algebra and arithmetic are correct.

1 point (clarity): The explanation is clearly written.

67.   ANSWER: The area of triangle ABC area is four times the area of triangle DEF.
        The perimeter of triangle ABC is twice the perimeter of triangle DEF.

        SOLUTION: You are using the midpoints of the larger triangle to construct the smaller one.
        Therefore, the base and height of smaller triangle are each half those of the larger triangle. Area
        of a triangle is $\dfrac{bh}{2}$. So, the area of the smaller triangle is $\left(\dfrac{b}{2}\right)\left(\dfrac{h}{2}\right)\left(\dfrac{1}{2}\right) = \dfrac{bh}{8}$, which is $\dfrac{1}{4}$
        of $\dfrac{bh}{2}$. Each side of the larger triangle is constructed of two segments of equal length. Therefore,
        the big triangle perimeter is constructed of three pairs of congruent segments. Therefore, the
        perimeter of the smaller triangle is $\dfrac{1}{2}$ the perimeter of the larger triangle.

        3 possible points
        1 point (content): Realize areas are in a 4:1 ratio.
        1 point (content): Realize the perimeters are in a 2:1 ratio.
        1 point (clarity): The explanation is clearly written.

68.   ANSWER: 100 square units.

        SOLUTION: Since each rectangle has a perimeter of 20 units, $2w + 2l = 20$, or the length plus
        the width $(l + w) = 10$ for each rectangle. The side length of the square is $l + w$, which $= 10$.
        Therefore the area of the square is 100.

        2 possible points
        1 point (content): Realize 10 is the side length of the square.
        1 point (clarity): The explanation is clearly written.

69.   ANSWER: 56 m.

        SOLUTION: Let ABCD be the vertices of the rhombus. Let s be the length of each side. Let X
        be the point of intersection of the diagonals.

        Triangles ABD, BCD, ADC, and DAB are all isosceles.
        So ∠BAC is congruent to ∠BCA,
        ∠CBD is congruent to ∠CDB,
        ∠DAC is congruent to ∠DCA, and
        ∠ABD is congruent to ∠ADB.
        By using SAS (Side, Angle, Side) theorem, we know that ΔABX is congruent to ΔCBX is
        congruent to ΔCDX is congruent to ΔADX.
        Therefore∠AXB is congruent to ∠BXC is congruent to ∠CXD is congruent to ∠AXD. Since the
        sum of these angles is 360°, all four angles must be 90°, making each of these triangles a right
        triangle and X is the midpoint of each of the diagonals.
        Therefore, each triangle has legs of length 6 m and 8 m, so the hypotenuse of each triangle,
        which is s, is 10 m. Therefore the perimeter of the rhombus is 40 m.
        The area of the rhombus is four times the area of any of the four congruent triangles, which is

$(4)\left(\dfrac{1}{2}\right)(6)(8) = 4(24) = 96$ sq. m.

$96 - 40 = 56.$

ALTERNATE SOLUTION: If you have properties of a rhombus, then $\overline{AC}$ and $\overline{BD}$ are perpendicular bisectors of each other, making all four small triangles congruent to each other. Sides of the rhombus can be found, using the Pythagoran theorem, to be 10 m each, so the perimeter of the rhombus is 40 m. The area of one small triangle is $\dfrac{(6)(8)}{2} = 24$ sq m. The area of the rhombus is four times that or 96 sq m. $96 - 40 = 56$

70.   ANSWER: About 58.875 square meters.

SOLUTION:

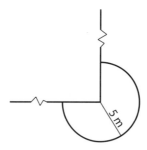

Attached to a chain, a dog could roam in a circle where the length of the chain is the radius of the circle. If the dog is attached to the outside corner of the house, he will be able to roam over $\dfrac{3}{4}$ of a circle, since the house will take up $\dfrac{1}{4}$ of the roaming area. The area of the circle ($A = \pi r^2$) is $(5^2)(3.14) = (25)(3.14) = 78.5$, but the roaming area is only $\dfrac{3}{4}$ of 78.5 due to the house. Therefore, 58.875 square meters is the answer.

71.   ANSWER: $72\sqrt{5} \approx 161$ square units.

SOLUTION:

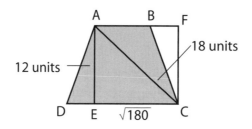

Altitude $\overline{AE}$ is a leg of right $\triangle AEC$ with hypotenuse $\overline{AC}$ and other leg $\overline{CE}$. Using the Pythagorean theorem, $12^2 + \overline{CE}^2 = 18^2$, or $\overline{CE}^2 = 180$, so $\overline{CE}\sqrt{180}$. Since $\overline{AD}$ is congruent to $\overline{BC}$, then the area is the rectangle formed by AECF, which is $12\sqrt{180} = 72\sqrt{5} \approx 161$ square units.

4 possible points

1 point (content): Realize triangle AEC is a right triangle.

1 point (content): Realize the area of trapezoid ADCB is the same as the area of rectangle AECF.

1 point (content): All arithmetic is correct.

1 point (clarity): The explanation is clearly written or the sketch is clearly drawn.

72.   SOLUTION: There could be several answers to this. Examples would be:

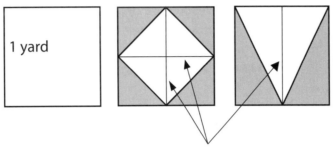

In each of the "windows," the bounding square has a side length of 1 yard. The shaded portions would be covered and in both cases shown, the new shapes are half of the area of the original square.

The center "window" is subdivided into four smaller congruent squares. In each case, the diagonal of that square divides its area in half, making all four shaded regions half of the original square's area.

The right "window" is subdivided into two congruent rectangles. The diagonal of each rectangle divides it in half, making the two shaded regions be half of the original square's area.

Care must be taken as solutions are submitted. For example, a "cross" solution could be given. While this is possible, the dimensions must be given. This one shown here is not half of the original square, which was initially subdivided into four smaller squares. The top left quarter square of the original square is subdivided into 16 smaller squares and only seven of the 16 are shaded, so the entire "cross" is not half of the original area.

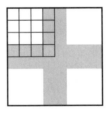

This "cross" could be altered to contain half of the original area.

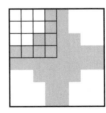

3 possible points

1 point (content): Dimensions are given correctly.

1 point (content): Computed area is half of the original area.

1 point (clarity): The explanation is clearly written or the sketch is clearly drawn.

73.   ANSWER: 22.36 units.

SOLUTION: $\overline{AD}$ is the hypotenuse of a right triangle, where 5 is one leg and $\frac{5}{2}$ is the other. This is the case for each segment of ABCD. Therefore, each side length of ABCD will have length $\sqrt{5^2 + 2.5^2} \approx 5.59$. Therefore, the perimeter is 4 x 5.59, or ≈ 22.36 units.

3 possible points
1 point (content): Realize $\overline{AB}$ is the hypotenuse of a right triangle.
1 point (content): All arithmetic is correct.
1 point (clarity): The explanation is clearly written.

74.   ANSWER: 15 units.

SOLUTION: Dividing the trapezoid shows three equilateral triangles each with side lengths of three units. Therefore, the perimeter of the trapezoid is 15 units.

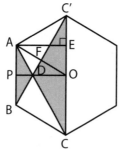

3 possible points
1 point (content): Realize the need to use equilateral triangles.
1 point (content): Arithmetic is correct.
1 point (clarity): The explanation is clearly written.

75.   ANSWER: $24\sqrt{3}$, or about 41.57 units.

SOLUTION:

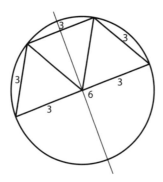

Assume that each side of the hexagon has length x. Label the center of the hexagon O, the midpoint of $\overline{AB}$ as P, and the vertex opposite C as C'. Since the hexagon is regular, segment $\overline{C'C}$ is straight, and $\overline{OP}$ is a mirror segment for polygon C'APO and polygon CBPO. Because $\overline{AD}$ and $\overline{BD}$ are congruent, D lies on $\overline{OP}$ and $\overline{PDO}$ is the perpendicular bisector of $\overline{AB}$ and $\overline{CC'}$. Construct $\overline{AD}$ perpendicular to $\overline{CC'}$. $\angle AC'O$ must be 60°, making $\triangle AC'E$ a 30-60-90 right triangle. Since a regular hexagon can be made up of six equilateral triangles, segment $\overline{AE}$ must bisect $\overline{C'O}$. That makes $\overline{AB} = \frac{\overline{CC'}}{2} = \overline{OC} = $ x. We know $\angle ADC$ and $\angle BDC$ are vertical angles. Therefore $\angle ADB \approx \angle C'DC$. Both $\triangle ADB$ and $\triangle C'DC$ are isosceles, forcing all four of the remaining angles to be congruent. Therefore, by Angle, Angle, Angle (AAA), $\triangle ADB$ and $\triangle C'DC$ are similar. $\triangle APD$ and $\triangle DFO$ are congruent 30-60-90 right triangles and $\overline{OD} = 2(\overline{DP})$ $= \dfrac{2\overline{OP}}{3}$. Since $\overline{OP} = \dfrac{\sqrt{3}x}{2}$ (hypotenuse of a 30-60-90 triangle is $\dfrac{\sqrt{3}}{2}$ of the side opposite the 60° angle), then $\overline{OD} = \dfrac{\sqrt{3}x}{3}$. Applying the Pythagorean theorem, you get x = $4\sqrt{3}$. Then the perimeter is 6 x $4\sqrt{3}$ = $24\sqrt{3}$.

76. **ANSWER: 144 square cm.**

SOLUTION: If you push each of the triangles toward the center of the square, they will form a square with a side length of 16. The area of the new square is 256. The area of square ABCD is 20 x 20, or 400 square cm. 400 – 256 = 144

77. **ANSWER: 832 units.**

SOLUTION: You must find the greatest possible value for a to determine the greatest perimeter. Set each side equal to the other two and solve for a in each case.
If 5a + 20 = a + 196, then a = 44,
If 5a + 20 = 3a + 76, then a = 28, and
If 3a + 76 = a + 196, then a = 60.
If a = 60, then one side is 320 units and the other two are 256 units. Therefore, the perimeter is 320 + 256 + 256 = 832 units.

78. **ANSWER:** $\dfrac{a^2 \sqrt{3}}{6}$ where a is the side length of the big triangle.

SOLUTION: If the big triangle is side length "a", a little triangle has side length $\dfrac{a}{3}$. Use the Pythagorean theorem to find the height of the little triangle to be $\dfrac{a\sqrt{3}}{6}$. That makes the area of one little triangle be $\dfrac{a^2 \sqrt{3}}{36}$. But the logo is made up of 6 of those little triangles, giving $\dfrac{a^2 \sqrt{3}}{6}$.

3 possible points
1 point (content): Realize how to find the height of the little triangle.
1 point (content): Algebra done correctly.
1 point (clarity): The explanation is clearly written.

79. **ANSWER: 34.72cm².**

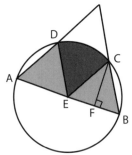

SOLUTION: $\overline{EC}$ and $\overline{EB}$ are radii of the circle, making $\triangle BCE$ isosceles. But, m$\angle$EBC is 60° because $\triangle ABC$ is isosceles. That means m$\angle$EBC is 60°, since $\triangle BCE$ is isosceles with base $\angle$EBC and $\angle$ECB. $\overline{CF}$ is an altitude of $\triangle BCE$ making $\triangle BCF$ a 30-60-90 right triangle (an altitude of an isosceles triangle bisects the vertex angle, so m∠BCF is $\dfrac{60°}{2}$ = 30°, m∠BFC = 90° ($\overline{CF} \perp \overline{EB}$), and m∠EBC is 60° because ΔABC is isosceles). The altitude of an isosceles triangle bisects the base too, so segment $\overline{FB}$ is 2.5 cm long. Side $\overline{CB}$ is 5 cm long because ΔBCE is isosceles. The Pythagorean theorem is used to find the length of $\overline{FC}$ (m($\overline{CF}$)² + m($\overline{FB}$)² = m($\overline{BC}$)², or m($\overline{CF}$)² + 2.5² = 5² and m($\overline{CF}$)² = 25 - 6.25 = 18.75 cm. Thus, m$\overline{CF}$ = $\sqrt{18.75}$, which is approximately 4.33 cm. The area of ΔBCE is $\dfrac{bh}{2}$ = $\dfrac{(0.5 \text{ cm})(4.33 \text{ cm})}{2}$ ≈ 10.82 cm².

Using similar reasoning, ΔADE must be equilateral with an area of ≈ 5.41 cm².

Since ΔBCE and ΔADE are equilateral, ∠DEC must be 60° because $\overline{AB}$ is a diameter and thus a straight line segment. In this case, the area of a circle is πr2 or (3.14)(25 cm). Thus, the area of the circle is ≈ 78.5 cm2. The area of sector DEC is $\dfrac{1}{6}$ of the area of the circle, or $\dfrac{78.5 \text{ cm}^2}{6}$, since the interior angle is 60°. Thus, the area of the sector is ≈ 13.08 cm2. The area of the region in question is the area of ΔADE + the area of ΔBCE + the area of sector DEC, or approximately 5.41 cm² + 5.41 cm² + 13.08 cm², which is 23.9 cm².

7 possible points
1 point (content): Realize ΔBCE is equilateral.
1 point (content): Compute the length of altitude $\overline{CF}$ correctly.
1 point (content): Compute the area of ΔBCE correctly.
1 point (content): Realize ΔBCE and ΔADE are congruent.
1 point (content): Realize the area of the sector CED is $\dfrac{1}{6}$ of the circle.
1 point (content): Compute the area of sector CED correctly.
1 point (clarity): The explanation is clearly written or the sketch is clearly drawn.

80. ANSWER: Perimeter 40 units and area of 96 square units.

SOLUTION: Since the diagonals form right angles and bisect each other, you have 4 congruent right triangles as shown below.

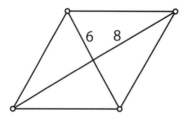

By the Pythagorean theorem, the side length of the rhombus is 10. This gives a perimeter of 40.

The height of a triangle is 6 and its base is 8. Therefore the area $\left(A = \dfrac{bh}{2} \right)$ is 24 square units for one triangle, yielding an area of the rhombus as 24 x 4, or 96 square units.

4 possible points
1 point (content): Realize rhombus diagonals are perpendicular.
1 point (content): Realize rhombus diagonals bisect each other.
1 point (content): Calculations and substitutions are correct.
1 point (clarity): The explanation is clearly written.

81.   ANSWER: Yes. Approximately 150.8 square meters.

SOLUTION: The length of each side of the fence is 13 meters, since $\frac{78}{6}$ = 13. Rover's chain is less than the length of one side of fence. Since each interior angle of a regular hexagon measures 120°, the area Rover can roam is $\frac{1}{3}$ of a circle whose radius is 12 meters.

4 possible points
1 point (content): Realize a hexagon has 6 sides.
1 point (content): Realize two sides of a regular hexagon form a 120° angle.
1 point (content): All substitutions and arithmetic are correct.
1 point (clarity): The explanation is clearly written.

82.   ANSWER: $\frac{1}{8}$.

SOLUTION: Divide the square into sixteen smaller squares.

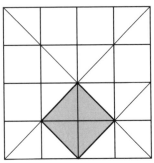

The shaded square is formed from four half-little squares, so its area is 2 little squares. The ratio 2 to 16 is $\frac{1}{8}$. (Note: The region can be divided other ways to generate the answer.)

4 possible points
1 point (content): Realize the need to subdivide the large square.
1 point (content): Realize the shaded region is comprised of 4 half-little squares.
1 point (content): The arithmetic is done correctly.
1 point (clarity): The explanation is clearly written.

83.   ANSWER: Approximately 122.7 in². Allow 122.7 to 123.1 in².

SOLUTION: The illustration below helps.

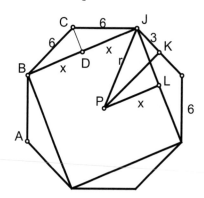

Using triangle PJK,

$$\sin 22.5 = \frac{3}{r}$$
$$r = \frac{3}{\sin 22.5}$$
$$r = 7.84$$

and from triangle PJL,

$$\cos 45 = \frac{x}{r}$$
$$x = r\cos 45$$
$$x = 7.84\,(.707)$$
$$x = 5.54$$

2x would be the length of the side of the square, or 11.08, and the area would be approximately 122.77 in².

NOTE – there are other ways this could be solved. For example, using triangle BCJ from the figure, $\frac{(n-2)180}{n}$ gives the measure of an interior angle of a regular polygon.

So,

$$\angle ABC = \frac{(8-2)180°}{8}$$
$$= \frac{(6)\,180°}{8}$$
$$= 135°$$
$$\angle DBC = \frac{135° - 90°}{2}$$
$$= 22.5°$$

So $22.5° = \frac{x}{6}$

$$x = 6\cos(22.5°)$$
$$= 5.54 \text{ units}$$
$$2x = 11.08 \text{ units}$$
$$A = 11.08 \text{ units}^2$$
$$\approx 122.77 \text{ units}^2$$

84.   ANSWER: 525.56 in2.

SOLUTION: Area of a circle = πr^2. In 6.5 hours, the minute hand completes 6.5 full circles. The hand passes over $(3.14)(5^2) = 78.5 \text{ in}^2$ in one hour. In 6.5 hours, it passes over $(78.5)(6.5)$ = 510.25 in^2.

In 6 hours, the hour hand covers half of a circle. One hour = $\dfrac{1}{12}$, so for the 0.5 hour, it covers $\dfrac{1}{24}$ of a full circle. The hour hand makes $\dfrac{13}{24}$ of a full circle in 6.5 hours. $\left(\dfrac{1}{2} + \dfrac{1}{24} = \dfrac{12}{24} + \dfrac{1}{24} = \dfrac{13}{24} \right)$ A full circle for the hour hand would cover $(3.14)(3^2) = 28.26 \text{ in}^2$. So, in 6.5 hours, it covers $(28.26)\left(\dfrac{13}{24} \right) = 15.31 \text{ in}^2$.

Combining the area covered by the two hands, we get 510.25 in^2 + 15.31 in^2 = 525.56 in^2.

Note, if the symbol π is used, the answer could be expressed as $(25\pi)(6.5) + (9\pi)\left(\dfrac{13}{24} \right)$ in^2, or $162\dfrac{1}{2} \pi$ in^2 + $\dfrac{39}{8} \pi$ in^2, which is also $162\dfrac{1}{2} \pi$ in^2 + π in^2. Expressed as an irrational number, this answer would be $167\dfrac{3}{8} \pi$ in^2. As a decimal, this would be 525.82 in^2.

If $\dfrac{22}{7}$ is used, the answer would be $(25)\left(\dfrac{22}{7} \right)(6.5)$in^2 + $(9)\left(\dfrac{22}{7} \right)\left(\dfrac{13}{24} \right)$ in^2, which is $510\dfrac{13}{24}$ in^2 + $\dfrac{13}{24}$ in^2, which is also $526\dfrac{13}{24}$ in^2. As a decimal, this would be 526.04 in^2.

The answers vary slightly because of the different values used for π. Other answers are possible. If a calculator is used that has a π key and the calculator is set for more than two decimal places, then the corresponding decimal answers will be slightly larger than what are listed here because of the increased value for π.

85.   ANSWER: 392 square units.

SOLUTION: The area of square BDEF is half the area of the right triangle inside of which it is inscribed, because if $\overline{BF}$ = 1, then the area of the square is 1 square unit and the area of triangle ABC would be $\dfrac{(\overline{AB})(\overline{BC})}{2} = \dfrac{(2)(2)}{2} = 2$ square units. So, the area of the right triangle ABC = 882 square units. If 1, 2, 3, and 4 denote the areas of the regions enclosing them, then region 2 = region 3 = $\dfrac{\text{region 1}}{2}$ and region 4 = $\dfrac{\text{region 1}}{4}$. Region 1 + region 2 + region 3 + region 4 = 882 square units. Substituting equivalent values of region 1 for regions 2, 3, and 4 gives

1 region 1 + $\dfrac{\text{region 1}}{2}$ + $\dfrac{\text{region 1}}{2}$ + $\dfrac{\text{region 1}}{4}$, or $1 + \dfrac{1}{2} + \dfrac{1}{2} + \dfrac{1}{4}$. Therefore, $\dfrac{9(\text{region 1})}{4}$

= 882 square units.

Region 1 = $\left(\dfrac{882}{1}\right)\left(\dfrac{4}{9}\right) = \dfrac{3528}{9}$ = 392 square units.

86.   ANSWER: $\dfrac{60}{7}$ square meters. There are many possible answers.

SOLUTION: Let x represent the length of one side of the rectangle with area 7. The length of the other side is $\dfrac{7}{x}$ and the rectangle with area 4 has side lengths x and $\dfrac{4}{x}$, whereas the rectangle with area 15 has side lengths $\dfrac{7}{x}$ and $\dfrac{15x}{7}$.

Therefore, the mystery rectangle has area $\left(\dfrac{4}{x}\right)\left(\dfrac{15x}{7}\right) = \dfrac{60}{7}$.

	x	$\dfrac{15x}{7}$
$\dfrac{7}{x}$	7	15
$\dfrac{4}{x}$	4	$\dfrac{60}{7}$

DISTANCE AND LENGTH

87.   ANSWER: 88 inches.

SOLUTION: $C = \pi d = \left(\dfrac{22}{7}\right)(14) = 44$ inches. But, that is the distance the roller moves along the ground. At the same time, the box is moving across the top of the roller and goes another 44 inches. So, the total distance covered by the box, in relation to the ground, as the rollers make exactly one complete revolution, is 88 inches.

        Note: if you use 3.14 for pi, you get 87.96.

3 possible points
1 point (content): Realize that the box moves the same distance the rollers do.
1 point (content): Formula use and arithmetic use are correct.
1 point (clarity): The explanation is clearly written.

88.   ANSWER: Approximately 22.507908 units.

SOLUTION:

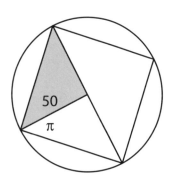

A circumference of 100 gives a diameter of $\dfrac{100}{\pi}$. The diagonals of a square bisect each other and are perpendicular to each other. Thus, half of a diagonal is $\dfrac{50}{\pi}$ and two of them (adjacent) are the legs of a right triangle with a hypotenuse of the side length (shaded in the figure). The Pythagorean Theorem gives $2\left(\dfrac{50}{\pi}\right)^2 = s^2$. Solving for s gives ≈ 22.507908 units. Note that the answer could vary slightly, depending upon the value used for π.

4 possible points
1 point (content): Realize circumference of 100 gives a diameter of $\dfrac{100}{\pi}$.

1 point (content): Realize the diagonals of a square bisect and are perpendicular to each other.
1 point (content): Algebra and arithmetic are done correctly.
1 point (clarity): The explanation is clearly written.

89.   ANSWER: 1.1968 or about 1.2 cm.

SOLUTION:

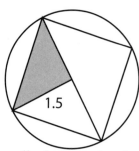

The diagonals of a square are perpendicular to each other and bisect each other. Thus, the shaded triangle in the figure is a right isosceles triangle with each leg 1.5cm long. Using the Pythagorean theorem,

$1.5^2 + 1.5^2 = s^2$, or $2(1.5^2) = s^2$.

$s = \sqrt{2(1.5^2)}$

$= 1.5\sqrt{2}$, or $\dfrac{3\sqrt{2}}{2}$

The area of the square is $\left(\dfrac{3\sqrt{2}}{2}\right)^2 = \dfrac{(9)(2)}{2}$ or 4.5 cm². Therefore $4.5 = \pi r^2$.

r^2 is $\dfrac{3\sqrt{2}}{2}$, which is about 1.4324. r is $\sqrt{1.4324}$, which is approximately 1.1968, or about 1.2 cm.

5 possible points
1 point (content: Realize the side of the square must be $\dfrac{3\sqrt{2}}{2}$.
1 point (content): Realize the area of the square 4.5 cm².
1 point (content): Realize $4.5 = \pi r^2$.
1 point (content: All computations are correct.
1 point (clarity): The explanation is clearly written.

90.   ANSWER: The distance between the two balls should be about 10 times the circumference of the ball representing the earth or about 35 times the circumference of the ball representing the moon.

SOLUTION:
Average distance from earth to moon: 384400 kilometers.
Circumference of earth: 39825 kilometers.
Circumference of moon: 11000 kilometers.

$\dfrac{384400}{39825} \approx 9.7$, which would round to 10

$\dfrac{384400}{11000} \approx 34.9$, which would round to 35

2 possible points
1 point (content): Ratios computed correctly.
1 point (clarity): The explanation is clearly written .

91.   ANSWER: 4 feet 8 inches, or 56 inches. Theodore can extend his tongue approximately 15.62 inches outside his mouth.

SOLUTION: You can create a right triangle using Theodore's mouth, the distance a person stands from Theodore, and the height of a person's nose.

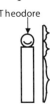

The distance from Theodore's mouth to the person will be 12 inches in length. Theodore can reach a person's nose that is 76 inches off the ground. This is 10 inches over Point D. Theodore's tongue will be able to reach a nose that is 10 inches below this point as well. Therefore, Theodore can lick a nose that is 56 inches off the ground.

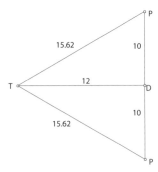

Theodore's tongue length outside his mouth is the hypotenuse of the right triangle. The hypotenuse, C, can be found using the Pythagorean theorem $12^2 + 10^2 = (TP)^2$, so TP= approximately 15.62 inches.

92.   ANSWER: Approximately 49.6 units.

SOLUTION: Triangle ABC is equilateral, which means that $\overline{AD}$ bisects $\overline{BC}$.

Since $\triangle ABD$ is a 30-60-90 triangle, $\overline{AD} = \dfrac{75\sqrt{3}}{2}$ and $\overline{BD} = \dfrac{75}{2}$.

Since E is the midpoint of $\overline{AD}$, $\overline{DE} = \dfrac{75\sqrt{3}}{4}$.

$\triangle BDE$ is a right triangle, so
$\overline{BE}^2 = \overline{BD}^2 + \overline{DE}^2$

$$\overline{BE}^2 = \left(\frac{75}{2}\right)^2 + \left(\frac{75\sqrt{3}}{4}\right)^2$$

$$\overline{BE}^2 = 75^2 \times \left(\left(\frac{1}{2}\right)^2 + \left(\frac{\sqrt{3}}{4}\right)^2\right) \text{ (factoring out } (75)^2)$$

$$\overline{BE}^2 = (75)^2 \times \left(\frac{1}{4} + \frac{3}{16}\right)$$

$$\overline{BE}^2 = (75)^2 \times \left(\frac{7}{16}\right)$$

$$\overline{BE} = \frac{75\sqrt{7}}{4} \text{ or about } 49.6.$$

93.   ANSWER: 29 meters.

SOLUTION: The longest segment will be the interior diagonal of the box, which is from point A to point B in the diagram below. Triangle ABC is a right triangle. The length of $\overline{BC}$ is found by using the Pythagorean theorem for $\triangle BCD$. $144 + 256 = 400$. Therefore $\overline{BC} = 20$. Then $\overline{AB}^2 = 400 + 441 = 841$. Therefore, $\overline{AB} = 29$ meters.

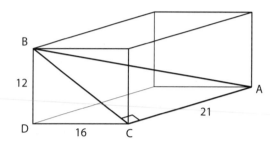

ALTERNATE SOLUTION: Using the diagonal of a box formula, where l represents the length of the box, w represents the width of the box, and h represents the height of the box.

$$d = \sqrt{l^2 + w^2 + h^2}$$
$$= \sqrt{12^2 + 16^2 + 21^2}$$
$$= \sqrt{144 + 256 + 441}$$
$$= \sqrt{841}$$
$$= 29$$

4 possible points
1 point (content): Realize $\overline{AB}$ is the greatest length.
1 point (content): Realize ABC is a right triangle.
1 point (content): All arithmetic is correct.
1 point (clarity): The explanation is clearly written.

94.   ANSWER: Maximum 13.4164 inches.   Minimum 2 inches.
SOLUTION:

1st move – K to 1 (or 4)   1st move – K to 1
2nd move – K to 2 (or 5)   2nd move – K to 2
3rd move – K to 3 (or 6)   3rd move – K to 3

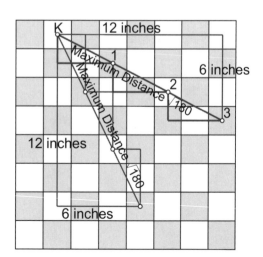

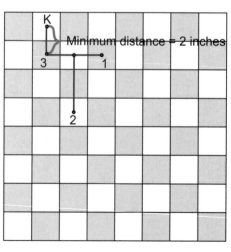

4 possible points
1 point (content): Maximum distance shown correctly.
1 point (content): Minimum distance shown correctly.
1 point (content): Computations correct.
1 point (clarity): The explanation is clearly written.

$$\text{Maximum distance} = \sqrt{12^2 + 6^2}$$
$$= \sqrt{180}$$
$$\approx 13.4164 \text{ inches}$$

95.   ANSWER: Square root of 3, or about 1.73 units.

SOLUTION: $\triangle CDF$ is equilateral as well because $\triangle ABC$ is equilateral, which means that $\overline{CD}$ and $\overline{CF}$ must be 1 unit. This also means that $\angle CDF = \angle CFD$. Since $\angle BCA = 60°$ (because $\triangle ABC$ is equilateral), all angles for $\triangle CDF$ must equal 60°. Since $\angle ACB$ and $\angle ABC = 60°$ and $\triangle CDF$ is equilateral, $\overline{FD}$ and $\overline{AB}$ are parallel. This also means that BEDF is a parallelogram. Since $\angle ABC = 60°$, then $\dfrac{BE}{BF} = \cos(ABC) = 0.5$, which $= \cos 60°$. Therefore, $\triangle BEF$ is a right triangle. Then, using the Pythagorean theorem, $1^2 + \overline{EF}^2 = 2^2$. Then $\overline{EF}^2 = 3$ and $\overline{EF} = \sqrt{3} = 1.7321$.

96.   ANSWER: 95 cm.

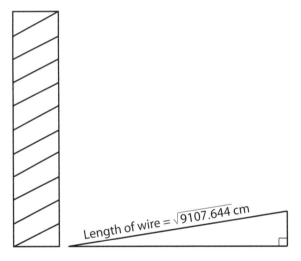

Length of wire = $\sqrt{9107.644}$ cm

SOLUTION: Visualize rolling the wire out flat. You would have a triangle that is 10 circumferences long and 15 cm high.
$C = \pi d = 3\pi = \text{circumference} = 3(3.1415927 \text{ cm}) = 9.424778 \text{ cm}$
9.424778 cm x10 = 94.24778 cm, the base of the triangle.
The height of the triangle would be 15 cm.
Using the Pythagorean theorem and adding the squares of the base and height gives 9107.644, the square of the length of the hypotenuse of the triangle.
The square root of 9107.644 = 95.433977, which rounds to 95 cm.

3 possible points
1 point (content): Realize the base of the triangle is 10 times the circumference.
1 point (content): Calculations are done correctly.
1 point (clarity): The explanation is clearly written.

97.   ANSWER: 362.8 cm.

SOLUTION: Construct a line segment between two of the three centers. Construct perpendiculars to the line segment at each center. The chain leaves each sprocket at the point where each line intersects the edge of each sprocket, so the distance the chain must travel between each sprocket (not on the sprocket) is the same as the distance between the centers, or 3 in. Now what about the distance traveled on the sprockets? For a three-sprocket system in an equilateral triangle configuration, the chain is in contact with each sprocket for 120°. So the chain is in contact with sprockets for 360°. So the distance around the sprockets is the circumference of a sprocket. C = $2\pi r = 2\pi 10 = 62.8$ cm. So the total length of the chain needed is 3.628 m, or 362.8 cm. (1 m = 100 cm)

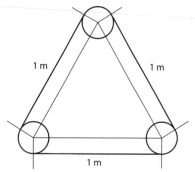

4 possible points
1 point (content): Realize that the straight sections of chain are 3 m long.
1 point (content): Realize that the three curved sections total one complete circle.
1 point (content): Formulas and computations used correctly.
1 point (clarity): The explanation is clearly written.

98.   ANSWER: 5 feet and 5.5 inches, or 65.5 inches.

SOLUTION: Five boards leave 4 spans of 16 inches each, totaling 64 inches. That leaves a half of a 2 x 4 at each end of the span, which adds 2(0.75) = 1.5 inches. Thus, the grand total is 64 + 1.5 = 65.5 inches (5 feet and 5.5 inches) for the total length of the wall.

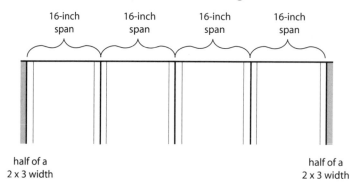

4 possible points
1 point (content): Realize four 16-inch spans.
1 point (content): Realize a half 2 x 4 left at each end.
1 point (content): Arithmetic is correct.
1 point (clarity): The explanation is clearly written.

99. SOLUTION:

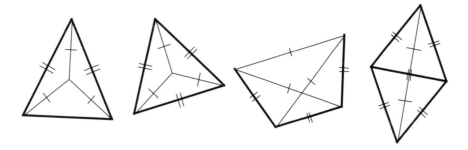

5 possible points
1 point (content): Isosceles triangle.
1 point (content): Equilateral triangle.
1 point (content): Isosceles trapezoid.
1 point (content): Rhombus.
1 point (clarity): The explanation is clearly written.

100. ANSWER: $12\sqrt{3} + 14\pi$, or 64.76690684 – NOTE: answers might vary depending upon values used for square root of 3 and π.

SOLUTION: The shortest length consists of two external tangents and two 120° arcs around the poles. The small arc would be 120/360 of the respective circumference, or $\left(\dfrac{120}{360}\right)(2)(\pi)(3) = 2\pi$. The large arc would be $\dfrac{240}{360}$ of the large circumference, or $\left(\dfrac{120}{360}\right)(2)(\pi)(9) = 12\pi$. The straight segments between the points of tangency would each be $6\sqrt{3}$, or $12\sqrt{3}$ for both. So you have $2\pi + 12\pi + 12\sqrt{3}$.

4 possible points
1 point (content): Realize the amount to be used from each arc.
1 point (content): Realize the lengths of each straight segment.
1 point (content): Arithmetic done correctly.
1 point (clarity): The explanation is clearly written.

VOLUME AND SURFACE AREA

101. ANSWER: Will vary.

4 possible points
1 point (content): Measurements are correct.
1 point (content): Proportions are set up correctly.
1 point (content): Arithmetic is correct.
1 point (clarity): The explanation is clearly written.

102. SOLUTION: It is assumed that the depth of the cake is constant. Divide the cake by drawing the diagonals of the square top. Subdivide each side of the cake into four congruent segments. Each of these triangles has the same base (the side of the square was divided into four congruent parts) and height (distance from the side of the cake to the intersection of the diagonals), so all the triangles on the top of the cake will have the same area. Since the depth of the cake is assumed to be constant, the volume of each piece must be the same.

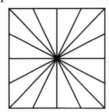

Note that this same discussion holds true for cutting the cake into any multiple of four (4, 8, 12, 16, 20, . . .) pieces.

4 possible points
1 point (content): Realize need for congruent triangles.
1 point (content): Realize need to quarter by major diagonal.
1 point (content): Realize need to subdivide each side into congruent segments.
1 point (clarity): The explanation is clearly written or the sketch is clearly drawn.

103. ANSWER: 2052π square cm or approximately 6446.55 square cm. This answer could vary with the value used for π.

SOLUTION: The sides of the cake's tier sides are cylinders, each with surface areas of πdh for a total of $\pi(60)(8) + \pi(48)(8) + \pi(36)(8) = 1152\pi$ square cm. Now we must account for the surface area of tops of each tier that must be iced. The entire top tier must be iced or $\pi r^2 = (18)^2$. The top surface area of the second tier will be $\pi(24)^2 - \pi(18)^2 = \pi((24)^2 - (18)^2)$ and the top surface area of the bottom tier will be $\pi(30)\ 2 - \pi(24)\ 2 = \pi((30)\ 2 - (24)\ 2)$. The total area to be frosted of all tier tops will be $\pi(18)\ 2 + \pi((24)\ 2 - (18)\ 2) + \pi((30)\ 2 - (24)\ 2) = 900\pi$ sq. cm.
The total is $1152\pi + 900\pi$.

104. ANSWER: 216 cubes.

SOLUTION: There are 8 cubes (corners) with paint on 3 faces. That means there are 64 cubes with no paint on them. They would come from a cube that is 4 units wide, high, and deep. In order to create that center cube, the original one has to be 2 units bigger (one unit beyond each face of the central 4 by cube) in each direction, giving a 6 by 6 by 6 original cube.

The figure shows the center 4 by 4 by 4 cube shaded. The non-shaded part shows a one unit wide layer added to the left. That new layer is also one unit higher, one unit lower, one unit in front of, and one unit behind the 4 by 4 by 4 cube. When the rest of the layers would be added, the new cube would be 6 by 6 by 6.

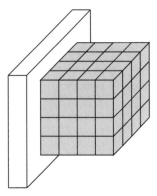

3 possible points
1 point (content): Realize that the center (no paint) is a 4x4x4 cube.
1 point (content): Realize 2 units must be added to each dimension.
1 point (clarity): The explanation is clearly written.

105. ANSWER: 260,000,000 cm^3.

SOLUTION: Much of the information in this problem is not needed. The volume of the portion of the pipe that is submerged is equal to the water displaced, which is represented by the rectangular solid with dimensions 20,000 cm x 10,000 cm x 0.65 cm = 130,000,000 cm^3. But since only half of the pipe is submerged, the volume of the entire pipe is 130,000,000 cm^3 x 2 = 260,000,000 cm^3.

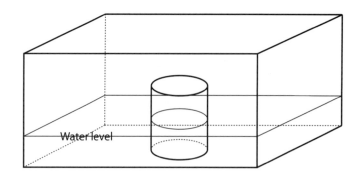

3 possible points
1 point (content): Realize there is extraneous information.
1 point (content): Calculations and substitutions are correct (wiith correct units).
1 point (clarity): The explanation is clearly written.

106. ANSWER: 536 square meters.

SOLUTION: Before gluing, the total surface area is the sum of the surface area of the three cubes, or $6(2^2 + 6^2 + 8^2) = 6(4 + 36 + 64) = 6(104) = 624$ square meters.

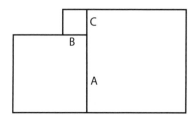

When glued as shown in the figure:
At point A, you lose 2(36) = 72 square meters.
At point B, you lose 2(4) = 8 square meters.
At point C, you lose 2(4) = 8 square meters, so a total of 72 + 8 + 8 square meters are lost when the cubes are glued together, leaving 536 square meters (624 − (72 + 8 + 8)).

4 possible points
1 point (content): Realize the need to start with the total surface area.
1 point (content): Realize that two 36 m² surfaces are lost at point A.
1 point (content): Realize that four 4 m² surfaces are lost using points B & C.
1 point (clarity): The explanation is clearly written.

107. ANSWER: Decreased by approximately 12 percent.

SOLUTION: Let r be the radius and h be the height of the original can, which gives a volume of the can $V = \pi r^2 h$. The height of the new can is a 30% increase over the original height, meaning the height of the tall can will be 1.3h. Let R be the radius of the tall can. Therefore, $\pi r^2 h = \pi R^2(1.3)h$. Solving yields $r^2 = 1.3R^2$ or $R = \sqrt{\dfrac{r^2}{1.3}} \approx \dfrac{r}{1.14}$ so R is about $\dfrac{1}{1.14}$ or 0.88r, meaning the original radius must be decreased by approximately 12 percent.

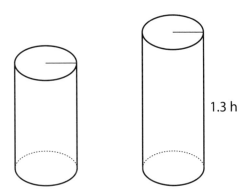

1.3 h

3 possible points
1 point (content): Realize tall height is 1.3 original height.
1 point (content): arithmetic done correctly.
1 point (clarity): The explanation is clearly written.

108. ANSWER: $S = \dfrac{\sqrt{CX}}{X} + 2X$, or $\sqrt{\dfrac{C}{X}} + 2X$

SOLUTION:

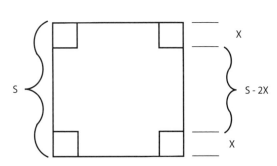

Side of box = S - 2X.
Volume of box = $((S-2X)^2)(X)$ (area of base times height).
Volume of box = C.

$$C = ((S-2X)^2)(X)$$

$$\frac{C}{X} = (S-2X)^2$$

$$\sqrt{\frac{C}{X}} = S-2X$$

$$\sqrt{\frac{C}{X}} + 2X = S$$

Simplifying, $\dfrac{\sqrt{CX}}{X} + 2X = S$

3 possible points
1 point (content): Volume formula expressed correctly.
1 point (content): Computations and algebra done correctly.
1 point (clarity): The proof development is understandably presented.

109. ANSWER: $\frac{1}{3}$ unit.

SOLUTION: The 2 glasses total 3 units. The 1-unit glass is half full of juice and thus contains a half unit of juice. The 2-unit glass is one-quarter full, so it too contains a half unit of juice. Together you have 1 unit of juice. Since the total volume is 3 units, the juice represents a third of the total volume.

3 possible points
1 point (content): Realize each glass holds a half-unit of juice.
1 point (content): Realize the two glasses represent 3 units.
1 point (clarity): The explanation is clearly written.

PYTHAGOREAN THEOREM

110. ANSWER: $\frac{20}{3}$ or 6.6666...

SOLUTION: If $\overline{AC}$ = 6 and $\overline{BC}$ = 8, then $\overline{AB}$ = 10 by the Pythagorean theorem. Using similar triangles, set up a proportion to find $\overline{DB}$. $\frac{4}{6} = \frac{DB}{10}$ or $\overline{DB} = (10)\left(\frac{4}{6}\right) = \frac{20}{3}$.

4 possible points
1 point (content): Solve correctly for $\overline{AB}$.
1 point (content): Realize the need for proportional reasoning.
1 point (content): All arithmetic is correct.
1 point (clarity): The explanation is clearly written or the sketch is clearly drawn.

111. ANSWER: Approximately 72.67 feet.

SOLUTION:

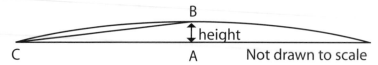

Not drawn to scale

Join the midpoint of the flat bridge (point A) with the midpoint of the bowed bridge (point B). Then, join each of points A and B with bridge endpoint C, creating right triangle ABC. While hypotenuse $\overline{BC}$ is not exactly equal to the length of the curved bridge between point B and point C, it is close enough for this discussion. The measure of $\overline{AC}$ is 2640 feet (half a mile) and the measure of $\overline{BC}$ is 2641 feet (half of a mile plus two feet). Using the Pythagorean theorem, $2641^2 - 2640^2 = (\overline{AB})^2$. Solving, $\overline{AB} = \sqrt{6974881-6969600} = \sqrt{5281}$. $\overline{AB} \approx 72.67$ feet.

This sounds preposterous and yet it is true. While the picture does not show it (because of the scale), the bow in the bridge would be almost imperceptibly different from the straight distance between points B and C.

3 possible points
1 point (content): Realize the need to create right $\triangle BAC$.
1 point (content): All arithmetic is correct.
1 point (clarity): The explanation is clearly written or the sketch is clearly drawn.

112. ANSWER: $\dfrac{\pi r}{h + r}$.

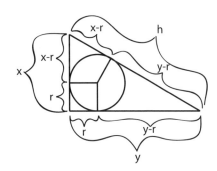

SOLUTION:

Since the circle is inscribed, radii drawn to the points of tangency will divide the triangle sides into two pieces. Each of the two legs will have one of its two pieces equal to r. If the legs are x and y, then the length of the legs would be r + (x - r) and r + (y - r) respectively. Since each of the vertices of the triangle is formed by two tangents to the circle, the hypotenuse will be divided into two parts too, one equaling x - r and the other y - r.

h = (y - r) + (x - r)

= x + y - 2r

Rearranging, x + y = h + 2r.

From the Pythagorean theorem, we know $x^2 + y^2 = h^2$.

From algebra, we know that $(x + y)^2 = x^2 + 2xy + y^2$.

Rearranging $2xy = (x + y) - x^2 - y^2$ or $2xy = (x + y)^2 - (x^2 + y^2)$.

$$xy = \frac{(x + y)^2 - (x^2 + y^2)}{2}$$

The area of the triangle is $\dfrac{(\text{base})(\text{height})}{2}$ or $\left(\dfrac{1}{2}\right)\left(\dfrac{(x + y)^2 - (x^2 + y^2)}{2}\right)$.

We also know from the Pythagorean theorem that $x^2 + y^2 = h^2$.

Substituting those values in $(x + y)^2 - (x^2 + y^2)$ gives $(h + 2r)^2 - h^2$.

So, $\left(\dfrac{1}{2}\right)\left(\dfrac{(x + y)^2 - (x^2 + y^2)}{2}\right)$ is $\left(\dfrac{1}{2}\right)\left(\dfrac{(h + 2r)^2 - h^2}{2}\right) = \left(\dfrac{1}{2}\right)\left(\dfrac{h^2 + 4rh + 4r^2 - h^2}{2}\right)$.

$= \left(\dfrac{1}{2}\right)\left(\dfrac{4rh + 4r^2}{2}\right)$

$= \dfrac{4rh + 4r^2}{4}$

$= hr + r^2$

$= r(h + r)$.

The area of the circle is πr^2.

The ratio is $\dfrac{\pi r^2}{r(h + r)} = \dfrac{\pi r}{h + r}$.

6 possible points
1 point (content): Realize the need to express x as (x - r) + r, and y as (y - r) + r.
1 point (content): Realize that x + y = h + 2r.
1 point (content): Realize that $xy = \dfrac{(x + y)^2 - (x^2 + y^2)}{2}$.

1 point (content): Realize that $(x + y)^2 - (x^2 + y^2) = (h + 2r)^2 - h^2$.
1 point (content): All algebra and arithmetic are correct.
1 point (clarity): The explanation is clearly written.

113. **ANSWER: 3 units.**

SOLUTION: The area of triangle is $\dfrac{bh}{2}$, so the area of ABC is $\dfrac{(24)(7)}{2}$ = 84 square units.
Triangle ABC can be divided into 3 sub-triangles each with an altitude of r, since the circle is
tangent to each side of triangle ABC.

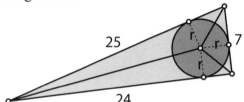

The sum of the areas of those 3 sub-triangles is also 84 square units. Thus, $\dfrac{7r}{2} + \dfrac{24r}{2} + \dfrac{25r}{2}$
= 84, or $\dfrac{7r + 24r + 25r}{2}$ = 84, which is 7r + 24r + 25r = 168. That gives 56r = 168 and r = 3.

6 possible points
1 point (content): Realize definition of incircle.
1 point (content): Realize that ABC is a right triangle.
1 point (content): Realize that ∆ABC subdivides into sub-triangles of radius r.
1 point (content): Realize how to compute the sub-triangle areas.
1 point (content): The arithmetic is correct.
1 point (clarity): The explanation is clearly written.

114. **ANSWER: 7 square units.**

SOLUTION: Perimeter = A + B + 6 = 14, or A + B = 8.
Squaring both sides yields $A^2 + 2AB + B^2 = 64$.
Using the Pythagorean Theorem, you also find that $A^2 + B^2 = 36$.
Substituting $A^2 + B^2 = 36$ in $A^2 + 2AB + B^2 = 64$ you get 2AB + 36 = 64
  or 2AB = 28
    or AB = 14
  or $\dfrac{AB}{2}$ = 7.
Since the area of a triangle is $\dfrac{\text{base x height}}{2}$ and A and B are the base and height respectively,
use $\dfrac{AB}{2}$ = 7 and say that the area is 7 units.

5 possible points
1 point (content): Realize A + B = 8.
1 point (content): $A^2 + B^2 = 36$.
1 point (content): Realize the need to substitute 36 into $A^2 + 2AB + B^2 = 64$.
1 point (content): Realize $\dfrac{AB}{2} = 7$ represents the area of the triangle.
1 point (clarity): The explanation is clearly written.

115. ANSWER: 8 feet.

SOLTUION: Before sliding, the situation is represented by a right triangle with hypotenuse 25 and one leg 7. Solving with the Pythagorean theorem ($a^2 + b^2 = c^2$, which gives $c^2 - a^2 = b^2$), the other leg has to be 24 (the distance up the wall the ladder reaches).

$25^2 - 7^2 = 625 - 49$
$\qquad\quad = 576$
$\sqrt{576} = 24$

When the ladder slides down the wall 4 feet, the vertical leg is 20 feet. With the Pythagorean theorem, the hypotenuse is 25 and one leg is 20.

$25^2 - 20^2 = 625 - 400$
$\qquad\qquad = 225$
$\sqrt{225} = 15$

Ladder was already 7 feet out, so to get to 15 it had to move 8 more feet.

3 possible points
1 point (content): Recognize the need to use the Pythagorean theorem.
1 point (content): Algebra and arithmetic are done correctly.
1 point (clarity): The explanation is clearly written.
Bonus point for recognizing that the triangle is a 3-4-5 right triangle so, with the hypotenuse 25 and one leg 20, the missing leg has to be 15 to eliminate the calculation using the squares.

116. ANSWER: $3\sqrt{26}$.

Solution: Since the hypotenuse is trisected, parallels through those points will also trisect each leg.

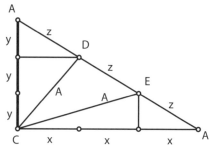

From the original triangle, $(3x)^2 + (3y)^2 = (3z)^2$ by the Pythagorean theorem.
And $9x^2 + 9y^2$ or $x^2 + y^2 = z^2$.
From the right triangle with hypotenuse $\overline{CE}$, $(2x)^2 + y^2 = 9^2$.
From the right triangle with hypotenuse $\overline{CD}$, $x^2 + (2y)^2 = 7^2$.
Adding the two gives $5x^2 + 5y^2 = 130$.
And $x^2 + y^2 = 26$.
So $x^2 + y^2 = z^2$ becomes $26 = z^2$ and $\sqrt{26} = z$.
$AB = 3z$ or $3\sqrt{26}$.

117. ANSWER: The figure is not a triangle.

SOLUTION: The smaller triangle part has a base of 5 and a height of 2. The larger triangle part has a base of 8 and a height of 3.   That gives different slopes for the hypotenuses of the triangle parts when they are oriented the same. Construct the hypotenuse of the big triangle and reflect the whole shape and you will see a small region that is not shaded. This region has an area of one square unit.

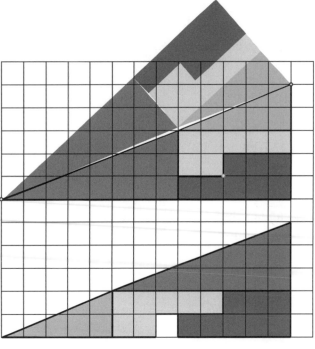

4 possible points
1 point (content): Realize the large and small triangles have different slopes.
1 point (content): Realize the "hypotenuse" of the big triangle is not straight.
1 point (content): Realize that reflecting the "triangle" will show the missing area.
1 point (clarity): The explanation is clearly written.

GEOMETRY PROBLEM SOLVING PUZZLER

118. ANSWER: The bear is white.

SOLUTION: Polar bears are white. By going south, west, and north to get back to the initial starting point, the tracker has to be at the North Pole. At any other location, after going north, there would be some distance between the end of the three-mile section the tracker went and the initial starting point. This could not have happened at the South Pole because the tracker could not go south first, as is stated in the problem.

Furthermore, polar bears do not live in Antarctica (South Pole). Polar bears likely evolved very recently (about 200,000 years to possibly as long as 500,000 years ago) from grizzly bears somewhere off eastern Russia or the Alaskan Panhandle. They are totally dependent upon sea ice for their primary habitat for getting their food (mainly ringed seals and bearded seals). As the world's oceans never have been frozen from the north to the south, polar bears never have had the possibility to reach the Antarctic. Polar bears are strong swimmers, but not strong enough to swim to the Antarctic. (http://pbsg.npolar.no/pb_faq.htm#antarctica)

3 possible points
1 point (content): White.
1 point (content): Realize this discussion can happen only at the North Pole .
1 point (clarity): The explanation is clearly written.
Bonus Point: Realize that polar bears do not live in Antarctica.

119. SOLUTION:

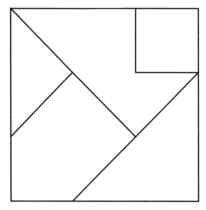

2 possible points
1 point (content): All five pieces are used.
1 point (clarity): The sketch is clearly drawn.

120. SOLUTION: Sketches may vary.

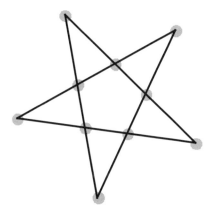

3 possible points
1 point (content): Thinking outside the box.
1 point (content): The trees are correctly configured.
1 point (clarity): The sketch is correct.

121. SOLUTION: Suppose your friend makes the first move in the game. You will answer by mirroring your friend's coaster placement. This is done by drawing an imaginary line starting at the center of your friend's coaster through the center of the table, and placing your coaster on that line on the opposite side of the center and the same distance from the center. With this strategy you will eventually fill the last spot available.

If you win the draw, the win can be guaranteed by placing a coaster directly in the center of the table so it cannot be mirrored. After that, the mirroring strategy would be used.

The assumption is that your friend does not know the strategy you have devised. If you both know the strategy, then the person who goes first will win every time. If your friend places a coaster so that the center point of the table is covered, you will not be able to mirror the move and thus would eventually lose.

3 possible points
1 point (content): Realize the need to mirror opponents move if the opponent moves first.
1 point (content): Realize the need to place a coaster directly over the center of the table if you go first.
1 point (clarity): The explanation is clearly written.

122. ANSWER: 4 times.

SOLUTION: If the clock is correct at 1:00 am, it will also be correct at 7:00 am, 1:00 pm, and 7:00 pm.

3 possible points
1 point (content): Realize the clock is right twice in 12 hours.
1 point (content): Realize am and pm.
1 point (clarity): The explanation is clearly written .

123. SOLUTION:

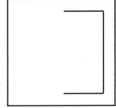

Fold on the vertical centerline and each overlapping figure completes a square.

2 possible points
1 point (content): Realize need to fold on the vertical centerline.
1 point (clarity): The explanation is clearly written or the sketch is clearly drawn.

124. ANSWER: Zero meters.

SOLUTION: Half of the cable length is 8 meters. That added to the 7 meters above the ground at the lowest point gives a total of 15 meters, the height of the pillars.

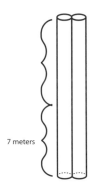

3 possible points
1 point (content): Realize only half the cable length is counted.
1 point (content): Calculations and substitutions are correct.
1 point (clarity): The explanation is clearly written.

125. SOLUTION:

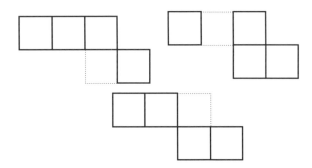

The dashed segments indicate the removed toothpicks.

2 possible points
1 point (content): Two correct solutions are shown.
1 point (clarity): The explanation is clearly written.
Bonus point: Show more than two solutions.

126. SOLUTION:

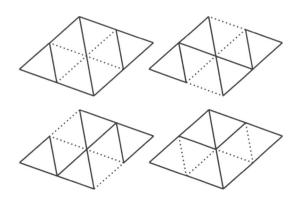

The dashed segments indicate the removed toothpicks. There are other solutions.

131

4 possible points
1 point (content): The figure is drawn correctly from the description.
1 point (content): Recognize which toothpicks to remove.
1 point (content): Show two solutions.
1 point (clarity): The explanation is clearly written.
Bonus point: Show more than two solutions.

127. ANSWER: $33\frac{1}{3}$ % of the original square.

SOLUTION: If the top right square is eliminated, one-third of the remaining section is shaded. One third of each subsequently smaller L-shaped section is shaded; therefore, one-third of the whole square will be shaded.

Alternately, the shaded squares represent $\frac{1}{4}, \frac{1}{16}, \frac{1}{64}, \ldots$ of the area of the original square.

The total shaded area equals $\frac{1}{4} + \frac{1}{16} + \frac{1}{64} + \ldots = \dfrac{\frac{1}{4}}{1-\frac{1}{4}} = \dfrac{\frac{1}{4}}{\frac{3}{4}} = \frac{1}{3}$.

NOTE that this initial ratio comes from the sum of a geometric series.

128. SOLUTION: From the fact that neither B nor C gives an answer, we conclude that both these kids have insufficient information to determine the color of their hats. Start with kid C who must be seeing at least one white hat on the heads of A or B (if C sees two black hats, C would know that C is wearing a white hat). Kid B therefore knows that B and/or A is wearing a white hat. Since B cannot give an answer, B must be seeing a white hat on A's head (if B would see A wearing a black hat, B would know B wears a white one). From the fact that neither C nor B can give an answer to the question, A finally concludes that A is wearing a white hat!

129. SOLUTION: There is one 8 by 8 square. Total number of squares: 204.

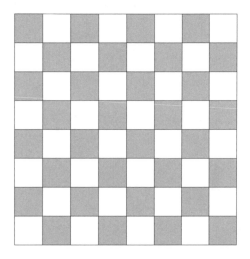
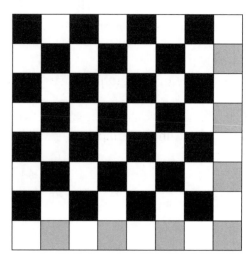

There are four 7 by 7 squares. Notice the right column and bottom row have gray squares while the rest are black. The big square holding the little black squares is 7 by 7. That is one square. Move the big square one space to the right and the left column would be gray and the rest black. That is a different 7 by 7 square. Now drop the black squares down one row (a third 7 by 7 square) and move it left for the fourth 7 by 7 square. By a similar method you will find nine 6 by 6 squares.

Continuing the process, you will find sixteen 5 by 5 squares, twenty-five 4 by 4 squares, thirty-six 3 by 3 squares, forty-nine 2 by 2 squares and sixty-four 1 by 1 squares. You might also notice the pattern of squares: $1 + 4 + 9 + 16 + 25 + 36 + 49 + 64 = 204$.

3 possible points
1 point (content): Correct answer.
1 point (content): Clear explanation of moving a smaller square on the larger one.
1 point (clarity): The explanation is clearly written.
Bonus point: Comment on the pattern of squares.

130. ANSWER: All related to pi. π^2, $\dfrac{\pi}{4}$, 2π, π written backwards.

131. ANSWER: Will vary.

SOLUTION:
Are the areas the same for each figure? Yes. Each has 5 congruent squares.

Is the perimeter the same for all 5 figures? No. All perimeters are 12 units except for the right-most one, which has a perimeter of 10 units.

Is 10 units the minimal perimeter? Yes. The figure shown has the least number of sides exposed.

What is the maximum perimeter? 20 units.

Can I get a perimeter between 10 and 20 units? Yes. This figure has the sides of the squares with a half unit overlapping, leaving a half unit extending each way, and giving a perimeter of 16 units.

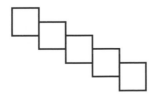

Can the six pieces be put together to make a square? No, 30 is not a square number and the six pieces have a total of 30 squares.

Can five of these pieces be put together to make a square? No.

Which of the shapes can be put together to make a box with no lid?

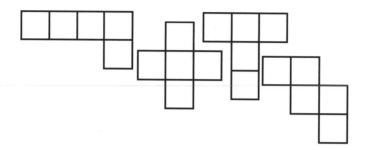

6 possible points
1 point (content): 5 questions.
1 point (content): Which ones form a box without a lid?
1 point (content): Maximum or minimum perimeter.
1 point (content): Will all the pieces make a square?
1 point (content): Any perimeter between 10 and 20.
1 point (clarity): The explanation is clearly written.

132. **ANSWER:** On the Equator.

SOLUTION: The east/west segments must lie on parallel latitude circles. Since the arcs on latitude circles are intercepted by two meridians (longitude lines), those arcs decrease in size as you move away from the equator, the two east/west segments must lie above and below the equator. Thus, the center of the desired property must lie on the equator.

4 possible points
1 point (content): Realize the east/west segments must be above and below the equator to have the same length.
1 point (content): Realize the north/south boundaries must be bisected by the equator.
1 point (content): Realize the center of the property must lie on the equator.
1 point (clarity): The explanation is clearly written.